THE CHRISTIAN METHOD
OF ETHICS

THE CHRISTIAN METHOD
OF ETHICS

BY

HENRY W. CLARK

AUTHOR OF
" THE PHILOSOPHY OF CHRISTIAN EXPERIENCE "
" MEANINGS AND METHODS OF THE SPIRITUAL LIFE "
ETC., ETC.

NEW YORK   CHICAGO   TORONTO
Fleming H. Revell Company
LONDON AND EDINBURGH

Copyright, 1908, by
FLEMING H. REVELL COMPANY

171.1
C693c

New York: 158 Fifth Avenue
Chicago: 80 Wabash Avenue
Toronto: 25 Richmond St., W.
London: 21 Paternoster Square
Edinburgh: 100 Princes Street

NOTE

THIS book assumes the positions which were dealt with at greater length in a previous one, *The Philosophy of Christian Experience;* and reference is made to that previous volume here and there. It is not meant, however, that those who are unacquainted with *The Philosophy of Christian Experience* will be at any loss in following the present pages. But they will have to take for granted certain things which are in the former volume more fully drawn out.

Incorporated in the following pages are some passages from papers which have at different times appeared in *The Expositor* and *The Christian World*. My thanks are due to the Editors of these journals for their kind permission to reprint.

H. W. C.

CONTENTS

CHAPTER.		PAGE
I.	THE IDEAL AND THE IDEALS	9
II.	THE ULTIMATE ETHICAL IDEAL	31
III.	THE RELIGIOUS PROGRAMME AND THE ULTIMATE ETHICAL IDEAL	54
IV.	THE CHRISTIAN CONSCIENCE	78
V.	CHRISTIAN DISTINCTIVENESS	106
VI.	THE CHRISTIAN'S RELATION TO THE WORLD	129
	(a) THE CHRISTIAN AND MATERIAL GOOD	133
	(b) THE CHRISTIAN AND THE SECULAR WORLD	146
	(c) THE CHRISTIAN AND THE SHORTNESS OF LIFE	162
VII.	THE CHRISTIAN'S RELATION TO HIS FELLOW-MEN	172
	(a) THE LAW OF LOVE	174
	(b) LOVE AND STRENGTH	193
	(c) THE CHRISTIAN AND JUDGMENT OF OTHERS	200
	(d) THE CHRISTIAN AND INFLUENCE	210
VIII.	THE CHRISTIAN AND DISCIPLINE	220
IX.	SUMMARY—THE INCLUSIVE RULE	236

THE CHRISTIAN METHOD OF ETHICS

I

THE IDEAL AND THE IDEALS

I

IT is a matter of common observation and experience that the Christian man finds it almost, or quite, as difficult as does any one else to adjust himself to a true position among the various practical problems of his days. Somehow or other, notwithstanding all the reinforcement of knowledge and of power which he would claim to have received through his entrance into the Christian kingdom, he is often utterly at a loss as to the course he ought to pursue. Whatever change may have been wrought in him by his faith in Christ has not enabled him to discern —still less to carry out—the true programme in all the emergencies of the common life. The inward processes whereby he became a Christian disciple seem to have left him much as he was so far as concerns his capability of setting himself right with experience as a whole: the adjustments of soul which he has made in obedience to the call of religion do not appear to count for very much in the way of inspiration when he stands face to face with the problems brought upon him by his life in the ordinary world; nor does he feel himself invested with any special power of self-regulation, beyond that of other men, amid the different sets of emergencies that are constantly presenting themselves to bewildered human thought. A religious settlement of life, in other words, does not seem to bring a complete ethical settlement of life in its train. Of course, the elementary virtues of truth, honesty, sobriety, and the rest are not referred to when this is said. These may be taken for granted; and, indeed, the Christian man would not expect, and does not need, in matters like these, to have any clearer illumination than that possessed by any one else. But these things are the mere alphabet of any practical and ethical scheme. And beyond these things, when life passes on into more complex, though not less essentially practical, realms—when it becomes a matter of finding the right poise of nature and the true line of conduct in affairs of a subtler kind—then the Christian man discovers that, precisely where he could wish to show himself possessed of a secret denied to others, he is as much in the dark as they. In regard to a right bearing in sorrow, in regard to the observance of a true proportion between the material and the higher interests of life, in regard to the maintenance of correct relations between man and man—in such matters as these, to take only a few instances, the Christian man feels himself in no position of decided advantage over the rest. He is, it is true, in possession of general principles which may cover a wider range and point to loftier altitudes than those held by many. He knows that all things are somehow to be made to work together for his good. He knows that a man's life consists not in the abundance of the things he possesseth, and that the spirit which is prepared to count all things but dross if heaven so ordains, and to take up the cross if the call shall come, is the spirit by which he is to be ruled. He knows that the law of his relations with his fellowmen is to be the law of love. But it is in the application of the general principles, in any given concrete instance, that he finds himself at a loss. Whether under a particular set of circumstances they call for immediate and positive action, and if so in what degree; by what line of conduct they may best be carried out; to what extent they are to be co-operative in the government of a special crisis; what is the mood and emotion they call for in order that, so far as they depend upon these things, they may not fail—the Christian man, after he has grasped his general principles, has still these questions to face. He finds himself as bewildered as the rest: indeed, the general principles he has acquired not seldom seem to be themselves the source of added difficulty, inasmuch as they complicate the case by setting the standard so high and thus imposing a greater responsibility and a severer test. In brief, the fact that a man has become a Christian disciple is by no means an open sesame for all doors. He appears to be in precisely the same position, in regard to life's practical problems, as those who do not definitely adopt the Christian attitude at all. He begins his working out of each sum, so to say, at much the same point as they; and, inasmuch as he has no book of infallible answers at his command, he is as liable as are others to be mistaken when all his calculations are done.

Yet the Christian man knows full well that this should not be; and he feels instinctively that for every one of life's emergencies his programme ought to be clear. Precisely because Christianity is so much more than an ethical system, it ought to solve—automatically, in fact—all ethical problems: it should possess, within that professedly all-sufficing ministry of transformation which it brings to bear on human life, a full range of ethical implications; and these implications should be easily discernible by any one who claims to have learnt the Christian secret and to have made the inward adjustments which Christianity prescribes. To enter into right relations with God (and this is what the Christian man claims to have done) ought to carry with it the attainment and the maintenance of right relations with the world, with all other inhabitants of it, and with every element of experience. The greater must include the less. There can be no such dualism involved in right living as is implied when the religious adjustment of a man's nature leaves him still at the beginning of his pupilage in regard to general practical concerns, brings to birth in him no reliable sense of direction amid life's tangled ways, and imparts no sufficient momentum to carry him past the sloughs and up the steep places and through the oft-recurring mists and glooms. So, instinctively, the Christian man feels. And, indeed, Christianity itself, as it has become articulate in its sacred writings, appears to take matters in the same way. For when it alludes to practical matters, to ethical concerns, to the varying crises of human experience, it does so as if by the way—never, of course, as thinking these things unimportant, but rather as holding that the Christian disciple's right self-management among these things may be taken for granted. When Paul declares that "all things work together for good to them that love God," he does so as if uttering a platitude, and as assuming that the Christian will know, in intellect and in experience, the truth of what he declares. When John emphasises the idea that " we know that we have passed out of death into life, because we love the brethren," the very form in which he casts his statement implies that a right relation to one's fellow-men ought to follow automatically from a right relation to the Christian gospel. And while exhortations to practical virtues do lie scattered thickly upon the New Testament pages, there are prescribed, for the attainment of power to carry them out, no programmes of self-discipline other than the spiritual programme whereby a man becomes, in the first instance, entitled to the Christian name,—the inference being that if that spiritual programme be sincerely observed, all is done in the way of self-discipline that even ethical perfection requires. The exhortations, too (it is worth noting, for the fact is a striking one), are always concerned with the simplest and most obvious duties, as if they had been constructed merely in view of the danger of theoretical Christian belief without real Christian life. It is not the *method* of virtue, but simply insistence on the fact that virtue will be there if the Christian profession be genuine, with which the writer—James, for instance—is concerned; and he selects, therefore, the more elementary graces for the pointing of his case. The larger crises of life, the subtler problems, the seemingly complicated emergencies

THE IDEAL AND THE IDEALS

in which the Christian of to-day so often finds himself puzzled, are, if dealt with at all, dealt with in the almost casual fashion indicated above—as though the New Testament writers felt that whoso had gone deeply enough into Christianity to care for a Christian bearing in such things as these would find himself automatically set into a true attitude as each crisis arrived. And all this confirms the Christian's instinctive feeling that his bewilderment, when he faces many of the practical problems of life, is a thing from which he ought to be free. It is not right that he should be thus compelled, when his relations to some element of his environment grow complicated, to begin all over again. It is not right that he should, notwithstanding his acceptance of a professedly all-suffering system of soul-adjustment, find himself without any advantage over the man by whom no such acceptance and no such adjustment of soul have been made. It is not right that the only thing his religion gives him as extra weapons wherewith to fight his way through the difficulties of a growingly complex existence should be a somewhat heightened emotion and a stronger belief that all will turn out well in the end. If Christianity did its perfect work, the Christian would be, not only in anticipation, but in actual present fact, conqueror over all, and would always be able to say, whatever the question of the moment might be, "This one thing I do."

II

The fundamental reason for the common lack of adequate equipment on the ethical side lies in the fact that the Christian's ethical programme is not sought for in the right way. The ethical or practical side of the Christian's life is looked upon as a thing detached; and it is not perceived that Christian practical ideals are rightly formulated only when they are translations into terms of practical life on the one religious ideal—that they ought to be, in fact, the one religious ideal dressed to play its part upon the practical stage. What we want is a unifying of our ideals—a unifying of them for the intellect, first, and thereafter, of course, an application of the all-inclusive ideal to each ethical problem as it comes up. We want to understand how one ideal includes all—how all ideals flow from one. We want to get at the varied processes of self-adjustment to practical problems, as the Christian man should practise those processes, by realising how they are inevitably implied in the conception of the main spiritual process, and how they really involve precisely the same movement of the soul. We want to see how the religious self-adjustment which Christianity calls for suggests and includes within itself all the minor self-adjustments required as experience passes on. The *minor* self-adjustments, they are advisedly termed; for minor, in the sense of being merely adjuncts to the larger and dominating self-adjustment, they would, in a true view of things, at once declare themselves to be. We want, at any rate, to understand that in addressing ourselves to the ethical question we are really addressing ourselves to the religious question—that the solution of the first is to be sought with the solution of the second kept in view—that the two questions are not two, but one. The ethical movement in any given case must be conceived as a special movement *within* a religious movement which covers all cases, a movement bracketed, as it were, within the larger whole. The true bearing of the Christian man among all the practical problems of his life is discovered only when we seek it away from the practical problems themselves, in the one spiritual ideal which the Christian gospel holds up. The ethical ideals should not need, for their investigation, a fresh start: they should be reached by a translation into appropriate terms of the religious ideal already apprehended. We need to perceive the ethical programme *bound up with* the religious, and the religious *suggesting* the ethical; and the mind should be conscious, in passing to and fro between the two, that it is but flitting from one apartment to another in the same house. We are on the wrong track so long as we merely try to carry over from religion into the ethical investigation some new spirit, some new mental or moral equipment, which will assist us, we hope, to carry the investigation through with success. All ideals are to be but translations or applications of the one ideal.

It is important that this should be understood. It is not, let it be emphasised, simply a matter of finding the practical consequences of Christian doctrine. To put it that way still leaves a break between the doctrine and the practical programme —a point at which the mind comes to the close of one investigation and takes up the next—indeed, the very statement of the problem in these terms implies that the bridging of a gulf between two separated things is the aim in view. And it is because this position is accepted that the ethical ideals of Christian men remain hazy, and ethical investigations are too frequently unsatisfying in their results. What is needed is not an acceptance of a gulf between the religious programme and the practical programme, followed by an attempt to bridge it, but an appreciation of the fact that gulf there is none. A study of the ethical side of life, from the Christian point of view, must start from the conviction that an ethical programme is reached, not by a process of more or less uncertain inference, but by a completer unfolding of the religious programme and its significance, and by a taking into the practical field of what that programme prescribes. The spiritual ideal and the ethical ideals should be given together for the inquiring mind. We want an extension of the field of the primary spiritual dynamic: at any rate, we want to see how the primary spiritual dynamic can be and was meant to be extended, so as to cover the entire ethical field.

It is clear that if this were accomplished there would be left nothing even apparently arbitrary in the Christian ordering of life. There would be an organic whole. Life would be no longer a set of unrelated activities, but would resemble a cluster of branches from the same stem. All the lines of action would be radii starting from a common centre: every programme of conduct, through whatever fields it might project itself *forward,* would run *back* for its justification to the same fundamental idea, and only as it proved able to do so would be declared correct: the many departments of activity, with all their differences, would be worked according to the same formula, and would fall into lines as parts of a harmonious whole. There would be no sense of disjointedness or jerk in passing from one practical question to another; no feeling that one is being transported into a strange land where the language previously spoken becomes unintelligible, and where the coin hitherto current will no longer pass. There would remain only different parts of one empire, the fundamental law of one being the fundamental law of all. Or, to change the figure, in the various sections of life's practice one would only be working different sums of the same order, employing all through the same method and rule. Nothing would be left to guesswork, nothing to experiment or hypothesis, nothing to hazardous ventures whereof the end cannot be discerned. Between all parts of life there would be a real relation. Back in the one ideal whereof all the subordinate ideals are but reduced, or particularised, expressions, would be the root out of which all the flowers and fruits of action grow. At all times, and under all emergencies, he who is striving for a right ordering and control of his life would have firm ground beneath his feet: no leap in the dark would he ever need to take: standing at the one central place, he would from there be able to touch the entire circumference of things. He would work with one tool instead of many. Instead of a number of lessons, he would have but a single lesson to learn. And not even under the most novel and startling questions which the sphinx of experience might propound would he be at a loss; for he would only have to fall back upon the primary formula out of which all subsidiary formulæ are to come, and could then, having discovered the word the moment calls for, pass safely on his way. With the ideals related to the ideal, discerned as specialised adaptations of the ideal, there would be unity through all the range of practical life; and that sense of coming as an uninstructed novice or an unarmed soldier to one ethical problem after another, whereby even the Christian man is too often beset, would give place to a sense that every problem is solved even before it marshals its perplexities, and conquered even before it throws down its gage. He who realises that every ethical rule is to be only a version, adapted to the occasion, of that highest rule in which the supreme spiritual adjustment of his nature is prescribed, will have this advantage over others—that while they must for each new crisis improvise a new programme, he has but to use the one programme, as giving the answer to the question of the new hour. For him the practical spheres of life are not elements in a disconnected series, but parts of an organic whole.

It may be objected that this is, in effect, the extinction of a Christian ethical system as a separate theme of study altogether, and that all thought about it becomes in consequence a futile thing. If all the practical ideals are given in the one spiritual ideal, it is upon that spiritual ideal alone that the mind should be concentrated. Why waste time in examining the outlying sections of life, when all their secrets can be read by reading the secret at the one central place?

As a matter of fact, a perfect spiritual adjustment of man's nature—a perfect ordering of life on the religious side—would, were it accomplished, make any study of practical problems unnecessary; and, as will presently be seen, the first thing to be said about a right management of existence is that on the Christian view there should be no necessity to take thought about it at all. Since the ideals are given in the ideal, an experience perfect in regard to the ideal must involve an experience perfect in regard to the ideals. The ultimate Christian conception is not that a man *should know how to bear himself* in any crisis of experience, and should act out his knowledge, but that he should bear himself rightly *without thinking about it*—almost as if he could not help it. There should be no need to particularise: the entire process of self-adjustment among practical concerns should be an automatic and unconscious thing. But, precisely because the spiritual adjustment is not perfectly made, the practical problems—which will not wait until the spiritual adjustment is consummated, but, pressing as they do, must be dealt with at once—

emerge into the field of thought again. Somehow they must be faced and conquered even while the soul is passing through all the intermediate spiritual stages towards the perfect thing. And hence comes the necessity of making a definite study of the ethical applications of the Christian ideal. The Christian man wants to put himself, at each recurrence of life's questions, into the attitude which he would have taken up automatically if the perfect spiritual condition had been reached. Only, in order to do this it is not enough to fix attention upon the perfect spiritual condition itself; for that condition, however clearly apprehended by the intellect, will not work out the practical consequences which it would bring about if it existed as an actual fact; and the Christian man must therefore take up the practical problems as they stand—remembering, of course, that the necessity of doing so is thrust upon him by the imperfection of his spiritual adjustments, and indeed finding in this very fact the way in which the problems ought to be solved. He may know that a right spiritual adjustment would result in an automatic right self-adjustment among all the practical difficulties of his days. But in actual experience no such automatic sequence is known, since its first term is not there. And it becomes the Christian man's duty, therefore, to discern with the mind what he cannot in its fulness prove in experience, and to ascertain how among life's practical spheres the perfect spiritual condition would be worked out. In the absence of a complete spiritual self-adjustment the Christian man can at least ask himself, face to face with all the various ethical questions of life, " What attitude, in this matter and in this, would the complete spiritual self-adjustment cause me to take up?" He must make two questions out of what is really one. He must do in intellect what, in a perfect ordering of things, would be done in experience without the intervention of intellect at all. He must make the transition in mind, since experience does not make it for itself, from the complete spiritual ideal to the ethical question of the moment, and must attack the second in the fashion which the mind has decided upon as being consonant with the first. And so we come back to what was previously stated as the main requirement in a study of Christian practical life. The ideals must be viewed as organically related with the ideal.

III

It may fairly be said that Christian ethical systems are not usually constructed on these lines. The ethical conception is not actually developed out of the religious conception, except perhaps in the sense of being reached by a process of intellectual inference therefrom—which, of course, means only that there is a passage for the mind from one to the other, not that the two are really one. The moral ideals are not *organically* connected with the spiritual ideal: there is no real identity (and it is no less than this for which we have been contending) between the adjustment of nature required from the Christian man in order to qualify him for the Christian name, and the ethical adjustments required of him as he deals with the practical problems of life. The majority of Christian ethical systems, while they may find in the main spiritual movement called for by Christianity a *reason* for the moral movements and attitudes they prescribe, do not treat these latter as being even ideally included in the first. They are not based on the idea that if the spiritual adjustment be fully and finally made, the ethical adjustments are *ipso facto* completed too, and that in so far as an examination of the ethical adjustments is still necessary it is necessary only because there is something lacking in the spiritual adjustment, and because man has consequently to do with two strokes what ought properly to be accomplished with one. The dualism which (it has been admitted) is temporarily inevitable is accepted as if it were not temporary, but were permanently inherent in the nature of the case. Generally, a system of Christian ethics takes this, or something like this, for its task—to find an answer to the question, What, if Christian doctrine be true, and the general principles inculcated by Jesus Christ be admitted, must be the conduct of a Christian man under the different moral problems of ordinary life? And this, it will at once be seen, is to perpetuate that severance, against which we have been protesting, between the religious and the ethical spheres, even though an inquirer is allowed or commanded to carry with him, as he enters upon the second field, a torch which he has kindled in the first. The whole thing becomes merely a matter of finding the practical consequences of Christian doctrine —which, as previously stated, is an inadequate method of regarding the task to be performed. The method assumes that, *after* the religious problem has been settled, the attack upon the moral problem has to be begun as something new. Ordinarily, the large generalisations of Jesus or of the New Testament writers are taken and applied, so far as they can be, to given practical questions; a bridge is built from certain Scripture utterances to precepts which (assuming the bridge to be soundly constructed) will be regnant over conduct in its various spheres; and by an extensive process of inference from Christian truth and from Christian revelation about the character of God, and about His relations with

THE IDEAL AND THE IDEALS 27

man, the entire field of human activity is supposed to be covered at last, and a sufficient rule provided for every emergency that may arise. But of course the further this process is carried the greater becomes the liability to error,—at any rate, the greater becomes the consciousness that absolute certainty is being left behind. For in this matter of inferring a detailed ethical programme, applicable in this instance and in that, from a general Christian law, it is not, be it remembered, simply a logical unfolding of terms that is being performed. If that were all, no difficulty would arise. But what is being done is an applying of general and abstract principles to concrete situations; and inasmuch as the concrete situations are almost always complex, composed, so to say, of subsidiary situations each one of which is capable of having a separate general law applied to it, the final mental act can hardly be called an inference at all. It is rather a balancing of diverse, if not opposing, inferences. Indeed, amid the complexity of life this process of inferring a programme of action from general Christian principles becomes not so much a process of reasoning as a process of guess. The guess may be plausible—may, as a matter of fact, come very near the mark. But it is a guess notwithstanding. And in a system of ethics so built up the final justification will be lacking for the mind; and it will be too much a matter of mere probability to give rest. It will be felt that upon the winding stairway down which inference has tried to find its road there are many loopholes at which error may have come in, and that what emerges at the bottom may perchance be error masquerading in the dress of inference, and not genuine inference at all. A system constructed in this way is insufficiently guaranteed to be relied upon with confidence quite unalloyed.

Moreover, besides that loss of the sense of intellectual security, which this method of constructing a body of Christian ethics brings in its train, there arises a danger of over-emphasis on one special place, of wrong accent, of exaggeration. Even assuming the method to be essentially sound, it could only be satisfactorily worked if *all* the general Christian principles were kept in view, *all* the elements of the practical situation held separately present to the mind, and, lastly, an entirely impartial judgment brought to bear upon the final distribution of sovereign power between the various laws themselves. But these conditions can scarcely ever be fulfilled. As was said just now, the last act in the process becomes, not a simple inference, but a balancing of diverse inferences; and it must be added that a quite unbiassed balancing of these is hardly likely to take place. Some one general law, some one aspect of Christian teaching, is likely to have, for the inquirer's mind, an authority or a magnetism over that of the rest; and in his formulation of the practical programme of life this is bound to tell, so that he will apply that particular law in season and out of season to the exclusion of others, refuse to listen to any qualifying voices, and in his zeal for one virtue do injustice to the rest. His ethical programme will be apt to become a monotonous harping on one string. Yet it is one of the most important requisites for the ordering of life, that we should know where the limits of each particular duty lie, as well as the line at which each particular duty begins; where one principle yields the sceptre, and another comes in to take the throne; how we may achieve a harmonious blending of the virtues rather than a shapeless prominence or predominance of one. That every general principle is to have its rightful authority, but is not to usurp more than its due, is itself one of the primary principles of true living. But on the method of Christian ethics which simply infers the laws of conduct from certain outstanding New Testament utterances of a general order, favouritism is sure to creep in and destroy the symmetry and proportion which ought, in a rightly guided life, to be shown. It is perhaps one of the most striking, and at the same time one of the most lamentable, consequences of constructing moral programmes as though they had essentially a separate existence from religious programmes, that the part is often taken for the whole.

The purpose of the ensuing studies is to attempt an ethical construction on the lines previously indicated as being likely to lead to a satisfactory result. No exhaustive moral programme is aimed at: indeed, some topics ordinarily included in an ethical scheme will probably be found wanting, and others not ordinarily so included will be found taken up. But some effort is to be made in the direction of relating the ideals to the ideal.

II

THE ULTIMATE ETHICAL IDEAL

IT may seem strange that the ultimate Christian ideal, in regard to the practical problems of life, should be the disappearance of those problems altogether, and that Christianity should look on those problems as being properly solved, not by direct dealing, but by their submersion in a larger thing. Yet the fact is so. The first thing to be said about the Christian ethical system is that, in its conception of the perfect ordering of life, it views man as not concerned with ethical questions at all, but as putting himself into such a spiritual adjustment that ethical questions settle themselves. It has already been stated that the New Testament, when it refers to the different crises of human experience, does so almost casually, as if considering that the Christian man's right bearing among them may be taken for granted. A perfect spiritual adjustment of man's nature would, were it accomplished, render unnecessary any study of practical questions: an experience perfect in regard to the supreme spiritual ideal would involve an experience perfect also in regard to all the practical ideals. That this must be the case the next chapter will attempt to show. For the moment we may be content with a simple statement of the fact. And it is with an appreciation of this fact that any fruitful study of the Christian conduct of life must begin.

I

The supreme spiritual adjustment of man's nature is performed in conversion; and to be converted is to be made out of the same moral material as God Himself, to be *made of good*. This conception of conversion has been elsewhere drawn out:[1] our present object is to realise what is involved herein on the practical side. Clearly there is involved in it an automatic right adjustment to every circumstance, an instinctive right bearing towards every question of duty and every temptation to wrong. "Instinctive" is perhaps scarcely the best word to employ, inasmuch as the automatic right attitude spoken of would result, not from the original endowment of man's nature, but from the working within him of that new nature acquired through the processes of spiritual experience from God and Christ. But, so long as it be thus guarded, the phrase may stand. To be made of good, just as it involves

[1] *The Philosophy of Christian Experience,* chap. iii.

freedom from all struggle within,[1] involves also freedom from all ignorance and perplexity concerning right relations with that which is without; and we are entitled to repeat that the ultimate Christian conception is not that a man *should know how to bear himself* in any crisis of experience, and should act out his knowledge, but that he *should bear himself rightly without thinking about it*—almost as if he could not help it. Just as, speaking after the manner of men, we may reverently say of God that He never needs to weigh and measure, to balance opposing considerations, to pause between thought and deed, so might one say of him by whom the perfect spiritual adjustment has been made, that he will under all conditions move straight upon the one perfect course, since it will be his nature so to do, and he cannot, consistently with the perfect spiritual adjustment he has gone through, do aught else. And the Christian ethical ideal lies in that automatic self-direction among all the practical matters of experience which would necessarily be performed by a nature *made of good*.

Christianity, in brief, sinks the conception of morality in that of sainthood. In the experience to which it looks forward as the highest there is little place for a mere resolve to do what is right and to avoid what is wrong; the Christian man

[1] *The Philosophy of Christian Experience,* pp. 59-61.

is not supposed to be drawing up schemes of virtuous living, ranking the various graces in their due order and apportioning to each one its rightful measure of care and zeal; he is looked upon, rather, as possessed by such high tides of spiritual passion, resulting from the inner condition to which he has attained, that the outward activities drop naturally into proper movement and shape. Christianity would have a man reach a stage of spiritual development at which it becomes unnecessary for him to concern himself with the character of the things he is going to do. The ethical requirement made by the Christian ideal goes far beyond a cold and commonplace morality, far beyond a mere assertion that the feet are not to slip aside from the path of virtue, nor the hands to give themselves to doing the tasks of sin. It asks for a permanent and passionate righteousness within, wherefrom a consistent righteousness without cannot choose but flow: it asks for such an established inner condition that all questions of conduct shall, by anticipation, be answered before they arise: it asks, so to say, that the *potentiality* of faultless action shall be ever present, guaranteed by the quality of the soul, and ready to be drawn upon whenever any crisis of circumstance presents its demand; and it declares that all the external processes of life are to be governed, not directly, but

THE ULTIMATE ETHICAL IDEAL 35

by the running of irresistible impulses out from the enduring state of the soul. A perfect ethical ordering of life is to be attained, according to the Christian ideal, without any fresh interposition of the will between the appearance of an ethical problem and its solution by him to whom it is addressed. To put it another way, the soul is always to have ready within itself, whether for the moment there may be or may not be some temptation or some question that calls it out to the open battlefield, such reserves as will make the result of any suddenly arising conflict a foregone conclusion. The Christian man's faculty of instinctive recoil from the evil or inferior course, and of adherence to the true course, is to be as much a part of himself as his faculty of sight or taste or touch; and the spirit of perfect readiness to move out upon the one right path is to be always alert behind the curtain which veils the secret of his personality from all save himself and God. The highest Christian ethical conception knows nothing of a constant choice, made with effort and perplexity, between alternative courses, nothing of a constant struggle in which the solicitation of baser methods is with difficulty resisted and the call of worthier methods half-reluctantly heard; and it knows nothing of a merely intermittent virtue which asserts itself at a moral crisis and then goes to sleep again till the warning trumpet of the sentinel conscience rouses it once more; but it declares for such an abiding condition of the inner nature as shall automatically secure the rectitude of the external programmes, and make the practice of virtue an entirely natural function, needing, at any given moment, no fresh gathering together of the forces of mind and will. That is the ultimate Christian ideal.

A reference to ordinary experience, on its practical side, makes clearer, if only by force of contrast, how great and far-reaching the ideal really is. For from the majority of men (whether or no the experience of even the greatest saints has ever reached the required level need not be discussed) this constant potentiality of a perfect ethical performance is too sadly absent; and it is not with a permanent bent away from all things evil and towards all things good that their characters are shaped. For the most of us our right doing, even when we do the right, is not the outcome of an enduring condition, the revelation of an embedded quality within. It is an affair of the moment,—in many cases almost an accident, one might say. At any rate, there were practically equal chances the other way. If the ideal be that we should have no need to concern ourselves directly with the practical ordering of life, since a right practical ordering of life ought

THE ULTIMATE ETHICAL IDEAL 37

to be automatically attained, then the language of the ideal is for the majority a foreign tongue. We drop into goodness occasionally. We pick up some of the opportunities of good that we happen to come across—and do not always do even that without reluctance. It may be granted that we have no passion for evil; but neither have we any abiding native passion for the best. Our natures, in regard to these things, are so largely neutral, colourless, indeterminate: we are midway between the passionate sinners and the passionate saints; and in regard to the established condition of our souls, abhorrence of evil is too strong a phrase, cleaving to good too superlative an idea, to describe what we are. At the best, our worthy activities, as each one goes forth from us, are the result of calculations freshly made. They were not inevitable. Other possibilities were not ruled out. And it must be understood that the ultimate Christian ethical ideal contemplates something more than that we shall come out unharmed and undisgraced from each crisis of our moral life, vanquishing every temptation by a sudden girding up of our strength, obeying every command by making a new call upon our powers—that it contemplates the existence in us of an abiding condition of good, out of which the practice of good must instinctively and inevitably come. According to the loftiest Christian ethical conception, the moralist is lost in, and rendered superfluous by, the saint.

II

It must not be supposed, however, that in thus removing the main emphasis of thought from questions of conduct, the Christian ideal ceases to care for them.[1] That there have been misunderstandings of the Christian ideal in this direction has to be admitted; and the fact that insistence falls upon inward potentialities rather than upon the outward manifestation of them has sometimes been taken (though quite inconsequently and without warrant) as if it implied heedlessness concerning practice. In the actual history of religious experience, at any rate, things have sometimes worked out that way, even though there has been no definite formulation of a doctrine to that effect. Yet a right understanding of the Christian ideal should surely be an ample guard against any danger of laxity in the external programmes of life. It is quite true, as has been said, that Christianity looks upon ethical questions as being properly solved, not directly, but by their submersion in a larger thing; but it does this only in order that the final issue in regard to those ethical questions may be raised to a higher level than any direct dealing could attain. Of course, if the significance of what

[1] See also Chap. V. Sec. 3.

THE ULTIMATE ETHICAL IDEAL 39

has been previously set down be apprehended, it will be obvious that this is so. What is demanded is that automatic self-direction among all the matters of practical experience which would necessarily be performed by a nature made of good. And this implies that practice is to be of the loftiest possible order, since out of a perfected nature only a perfect practice can come.

It is worth while to insist on the point, since in giving itself to those distinctly spiritual processes by which the inward perfecting is to be attained, human nature, with its limited powers of application and its readiness to shut its eyes, is apt to let other things slide. The inward perfecting once attained, of course the danger would be passed; but the mere *effort to attain* the inward perfecting may lead to laxity in that department of life which, were inward perfecting reached, would settle itself on right lines. The intellectual acceptance of the truth that the Christian ethical ideal demands a right external ordering, automatically issuing from a right inward condition, may result in that very imperfection of practice which the Christian ideal forbids. And indeed, one remembers how Christ Himself was careful to insist on the fact that His demands were, not less, but more, searching than any demands that had been made before. Face to face with the systems of His day, and substituting His own system for them, He realised, evidently, that the principles which He was declaring were so entirely different from what was currently considered to be righteousness that they might easily be misunderstood—or at least that in actual life their far-reaching implications might be forgotten. The Pharisees, for instance, might sneer because the code of laws on which they laid such stress found no place in Christ's scheme of things, and might say that He let His disciples off lightly. He shows, therefore, how deep-reaching His requirements are. There is something like a touch of sarcasm in it too. " Think not that I came to destroy the law or the prophets: I came not to destroy, but to fulfil." Not to destroy—that was really what the Pharisees were doing with the law and the prophets, in spite of their loud professions of loyalty to them. But to fulfil—the Pharisees, who had in a manner fulfilled them, filled them with all sorts of things they could not hold, had not fulfilled them in truth after all. That work was left for Christ to do. He was to " fulfil " all the moralities of law and prophets by His method of drawing the attention away from them; and the latter thing was only done with the first in view. And again, " Except your righteousness shall exceed the righteousness of the scribes and Pharisees, ye shall in no wise enter into the kingdom of heaven." *Exceed* the righteousness of the scribes and Pharisees—although the scribes and Pharisees already had some prescription of righteousness for almost every moment of the day! Christ was not going to have it supposed, either by the Pharisees or by any who might join His band, that the new preaching meant a lowering of the standard of life. It meant precisely the opposite of that. He took one sin after another which they of old time had condemned, and His clear "But I say unto you" rang out to condemn, not only the sin, but the thought of it, the spirit of it, whether or no the sin itself were actually done; and the implication was that in His greater and deeper demand the smaller and shallower demand was of necessity wrapped up. He took the emphasis away from external action, not to make moral distinctions unimportant, but to invest them with a deeper importance than they had ever possessed. Although He was not giving out a detailed programme of conduct such as the scribes and Pharisees were always ready with, He was imposing a larger requirement than they—a requirement wherein theirs, so far as it was concerned with a really ethical management of the outward life, was included as a matter of course. And the modern student of the Christian ideal needs to remind himself that the Christian ideal removes the emphasis of thought from the outward programmes of life, not because it has no care for them, but because in the greater achievement for which it asks they cannot but be truly worked out.

That ordinary experience had not always realised this has been already confessed. And it is not difficult to find some reason for the fact. Conduct is a tangible thing: it is, as it were, something one can see and weigh and measure: one knows where it begins and where it ends; and so long as it is definite actions one has to deal with, one knows exactly where one stands. A method of life which prescribes a programme of outward duties—one may be able or unable to fulfil the programme, but one will at any rate understand what is wanted. But in the realm of motive and spirit and character it is easy to get bewildered: an air of vagueness hangs round it all; and once it is said that the Christian method calls men to take their eyes away from conduct, because conduct is, after all, not the principal thing, bewilderment is apt to come back upon the external life, and thus in the realm of practice moral bearings are swiftly lost. Were we commanded to do this or that—well, it would be straight and plain. Told that it is not primarily with the issuing of such commands that the Christian method of life is concerned, we come, albeit unconsciously, to draw wrong inferences. We

THE ULTIMATE ETHICAL IDEAL

understand that arduous toil after correctness of conduct no longer counts as chief; and we read it as if it were the correctness of conduct rather than the arduous toil after it that has ceased to count. If this be a fine distinction, it is at any rate one which those who would live by the Christian ideal must strive to understand. If the imperativeness of law be abolished in one sense according to the Christian scheme, it is its *immediate,* its *direct,* imperativeness alone. That imperativeness acts still, though the perfected inner condition which the Christian ideal demands should cease to be conscious of its pressure and its curb. With all its insistence on an automatic right ordering of life's practice as the highest thing, the Christian ideal nevertheless has to say in regard to the law, that it came not to destroy but to fulfil.

It is—let it be repeated—because, even for the best, the realisation of the Christian ideal is only partial, that all this has to be said. With the ideal completely realised there would be no further need to emphasise the fact that, even in drawing the thought away from conduct, the Christian ideal recognises how important conduct is; for, as was said, out of a perfected nature only a perfected practice could come. The thing would prove itself simply by taking place. But in the transition phase of his spiritual experience man may fix his thought upon the religious processes he is called upon to go through, and forget that he must also keep in mind what, if those processes were carried through to their final issue, would adjust itself. Hence comes the need for a reminder that emphasis on that which is within implies no carelessness as to that which is without. We shall see at a later stage how a comprehension of the ultimate ideal is to guide man's efforts after a right self-adjustment to practical problems as they arise. For the moment the truth must be emphasised that, according to the Christian ideal, conduct is exalted to as high a place as any scheme of morality could give it. It is not exalted conduct, but the methods by which man must temporarily lift himself to the plane of exalted conduct, that the Christian ideal sweeps away.

III

According to the loftiest Christian conception, then, a perfected morality is by no means the greatest thing: the loftiest Christian conception looks on the moralist as lost in the saint, and calls for an abiding inner condition by which the rectitude of external programmes shall be automatically secured. The ideal is admittedly high —with something even of severity and sternness in the uncompromising requirements of it, one

THE ULTIMATE ETHICAL IDEAL 45

might at first be inclined to declare. Yet it is worth noting in this connection, that to make such a stringent demand as all this implies is quite in line with the Christian doctrine of the Fatherhood of God; and, with a little consideration, one reaches the seeming paradox that the very absoluteness of the requirement takes away its aspect of severity, and invests the God who makes it with the office, not alone of Ruler and Judge, but of Father too. Were God satisfied with man's attainment when no apparent tangible transgression rises up to offend His eye, were He content with a mere external conformity to an imposed law, then He would be Ruler indeed, but Ruler only, and the deeper relationship of Fatherhood would find no place. But because God's demands upon us reach further than that which is visible and outward, because He asks for much more than an external ethical perfection, He reveals Himself as connected (at any rate as wanting to be connected) in His own inmost character with ours, and stands forth as Father of our spirits, not only as Lord and King. For between master and servant, between king and subject, there is no question of inward condition at all: so long as the visible courses of servant or subject lead to no controversy and are approved as correct, the requirements of the relation are fulfilled; it is only within the limits of your own family circle that you can hold any inquisition into the secrets of character, only in those bound to you by closer ties than those of mere service that you can demand or expect a spirit congenial to your own. And thus, just because God, according to the Christian view, asks for this saintliness wherein all outward programmes are transcended, He declares us to be to Him in the relation of children in His family —declares, at any rate, that this relation is potentially [1] ours. The very depth and greatness of what He requires shows that He is more than a King seeking to exercise a despotic sway; for a Father, recognising that our spirits are come out from His, and beholding in us capabilities of character that mark out our natures as the offspring of His own—a Father, and a Father alone, could say, " It is in the inward parts that rightness must be established." The very fact that the ultimate Christian ideal is so searching proves that the God who sets the ideal on high counts Himself as being in, or as ready to enter, the closest relationship with man. The very ideal in which the greatness of the Christian demand

---

[1] *Potentially,* because the Fatherhood of God, while in a manner and in degree a reality for all men, does not come fully into play till man's right spiritual adjustment has been made. See chap. iv. in *The Philosophy of Christian Experience.*

THE ULTIMATE ETHICAL IDEAL

is embodied becomes also the revelation which announces the Christian conception of the grace of God.

IV

Over against the admitted stringency of the ultimate Christian ideal must be set the fact that it really means, in the truest sense, the emancipation of man. In accepting that ideal for the goal of his moral and spiritual striving, man moves toward no narrow prison-door, but rather toward a "large place." And, inasmuch as attempts are not seldom made, by a mere manipulation of moral laws, by giving to them all possible elasticity, by reducing their pressure to a minimum, to secure for man that liberty whereto he feels he has a native right, it is worth while insisting on the truth that Christianity in its lofty ideal of an automatic right practice, proceeding out of an abiding condition within, has found a more excellent way. Inasmuch, also, as from even the Christian point of view the true conception of liberty is not always grasped, there is further reason for laying stress upon it and making it clear. The greatness of the ultimate Christian ideal implies, as has just been said, the Fatherhood, actual or potential, of God. It implies also the true freedom of man.

The reconciliation of human initiative, human

freedom, the rights of personality with law, proceeds usually by the method of attenuating the demands of law to the furthest possible point consistent with the safety of society as a whole. The assumption is that adherence to direction and law is necessarily inconsistent with the possession of true liberty and with the consciousness of being free. Yet the reconciliation of liberty and law is possible by a quite different method; and Christianity, in its ultimate ethical ideal, makes the reconciliation between the two in its own way, saving the honour and the sovereignty of both. The assumption of inconsistency between adherence to law and the possession of freedom is fundamentally false. Freedom may be ours by reason of the absence of law, it is true, although anarchy rather than freedom is the word which better describes the condition of things resulting therefrom; but freedom may be ours too through harmony with law, through entire agreement between the inward movement of our natures and the prescriptions of law outside; and it is freedom such as this that alone deserves the name. The consciousness of liberty is ours, not when laws are silent, but when desire in us speaks with the same voice as that in which the commands of law are proclaimed. One does not need to look far for an instance. We know it for a binding law of the social state that no man shall steal another man's goods,—but does that law interfere with our sense of freedom? Not if we be honest men and women. Some members of the community there are who by reason of that law feel their liberty curtailed, because to steal another man's goods is precisely the thing they want to do; but the majority find no grievance in such an enactment, do not take it as any restriction or restraint. We are free, notwithstanding that we are not permitted to be thieves; and we are free because our desire and the law's command are at one. Freedom, in fact, lies not in the absence of law, but in our harmony with law. When law, command, direction, do not quarrel with what we are—when the movement of our nature is not in the opposite direction from the movement of law, so that discomfort and chafing and conflict result from the collision of the two, but in the same direction as that of law, so that in harmonious company the two work themselves out—then is our sense of freedom wholly unimpaired, let law be far-reaching and inexorable as it may. For through harmony with law the very consciousness of law disappears: it is not until we begin to kick against the pricks that we realise the sharpness of the goad; and if we have no desire to enter upon this or that forbidden way, we do not see the sign put up to warn us off. By our harmony with the law our freedom from the law is secured. Life works itself out unfettered if only its impulses be pure. Authority, then, has not to dictate or to forbid what life shall be or shall not be: it does but confirm what life is.

It is precisely this condition that is called for by the Christian ethical ideal; and it is precisely this condition, let it be added, that the Christian religion sets itself to bring about for man. Its aim is to set man free from the yoke of bondage. And it views all lower moralities as insufficient, not only because in fulfilling them (even if he fulfils them perfectly) man fails to discharge his obligations and to rise to the level he ought to reach, but because they fail to bestow on man the freedom to which he has a right. All systems of morality—however far they may be Christianised in their programmes, and however far they may depend for their effectiveness on Christian ideas, makes no difference—leave those who adopt them without the privilege they ought to enjoy. Christianity, for that matter, is at one with the most modern voices calling for liberty in declaring that freedom is the supreme prize, even though Christianity's method of attaining freedom be different from that which the insistent voices of the time recommend; and no understanding of Christianity is complete if it does not realise how in the Christian ideal the truest freedom is in-

THE ULTIMATE ETHICAL IDEAL 51

volved. Yet even from the Christian point of view this is not always understood, as was stated just now. There are so many ideas and so many modes of expression current in Christian circles by which the essential conception of Christian liberty (in the sense indicated) is obscured. Men are pointed to certain lines of action which it is alleged ought, if they be Christian disciples, to become theirs; and they are urged to take a hold upon themselves and force their activities along those lines. But even if they succeeded in doing that to the highest pitch of perfection, no forcing of themselves into any line of action could be anything else than bondage. To drill ourselves into obedience to words of command, even though they be Christ's, is not to be set free. The thoughts and phrases which circle about the conception of imitating Christ are also responsible for obscuring the view of liberty as it is contained in the Christian ethical ideal. Men aim at a sort of unerring mechanical skill which shall enable them to make each line of life's writing an exact reproduction of the line set at the top of the page by Christ's own hand. This may be the best bondage in all the world, but it is bondage still. It is possible to speak so much about imitating Christ, and about following in Christ's steps, and about making our outward doing conform to Christ's own, that the whole conception of Christian ethics grows artificial, and the experience of liberty passes entirely out of range. In such self-compulsion freedom, deliverance, is not known. To live by this method is still to wear the yoke. It is quite true that a man may have to begin with this; but if it be at that he stops, and with that he ends, he does not know the freedom wherewith Christianity would make him free. For it is from the contradiction between impulses within and law without that the Christian method, carried to its utmost height, is to emancipate the Christian man; and in its ideal of an automatically-wrought right programme, proceeding out of a rightly adjusted nature, Christianity provides for the best freedom that human life can know. In the realisation of that ideal the soul attains the elasticity, the sense of bounding joy, which it is apt to seek mistakenly by a mere loosening of the bonds of law when it seeks it at all, or which, under inadequate interpretations of the Christian system, it is so apt to lose. It is actually in the interests of liberty and largeness of life that the full scope of the Christian ethical ideal needs to be grasped. In the hour of attaining that ideal the consciousness of being pressed and oppressed by law is gone, and the soul, because it has no more contention with the good that binds it, is most truly free.

V

The ultimate ethical ideal, therefore, from the Christian point of view, is this—an automatic right adjustment to every circumstance, an instinctive right bearing toward every question of duty and every temptation to wrong. He who attains to the ideal will under all conditions move straight upon the one perfect course, since it will be his nature so to do.

III

THE RELIGIOUS PROGRAMME AND THE ULTIMATE ETHICAL IDEAL

IT may be asked, however, whether the programme which religion prescribes to man really makes for the attainment of a practice right through all its range. "You may advance as a *theory* that such a practice is the thing which Christianity holds desirable," it may be said, "but when we enter the distinctively religious realm, and concern ourselves with distinctively religious terms, are we really set upon the road toward this ethical ideal? Salvation and faith, and all the other terms which Christianity is always using—what have they to do with, and how do they further, a perfection of life on its practical side? How are you going to run any vital and organic line of connection from these religious terms, and from the processes they denote, to a perfect practice issuing from a perfect inward condition? It is all very well to say that Christianity demands a perfect practice—but does its primary religious programme have any natural bearing on the matter of practice at all?"

Certainly the question must be faced, if we are to accomplish what at the outset was declared to be a necessary thing, and are to relate the ideals to the ideal. It must be made clear that in concerning himself with religion, in taking up the attitude and going through the discipline of soul which Christianity ordains, a man is really doing more than this, and is really providing for an outward activity that shall be perfect down to its minutest detail. Religion, in brief, must be seen not only as *demanding* an automatic right practice, but as *creating* it.

And if the religious programme be rightly conceived, it is at once seen that this is precisely what religion does. It is quite true that the Christian programme is sometimes so formulated —faith and salvation, and all the other standard terms of the religious life, are sometimes so interpreted—as to keep religion out of all relation with practice, and to make it possible to progress in the religious life without coming any nearer to ethical completeness. A view of religion, for example, that is merely forensic—a view of religion, in other words, which simply takes it as enabling a man to stand in a position toward God legally blameless and clear—leaves the matter of practice untouched. Similarly a view of religion that is merely mystical—a view of religion which takes it as essentially consisting in an emotional self-abandonment to the presence and influence of God (whether that presence and influence be considered as acting from within or from without, and however that presence and influence may, according to the particular theory, be mediated, makes no difference) does not provide, except perhaps in some very indirect fashion, for an elevation of life's activity to the perfect level. But, with the religious programme rightly read, we perceive at once that to give ourselves to the Christian religious programme is to secure that automatic ethical perfection which, as has been stated, Christianity demands.

The programme of the Christian religion has been dealt with, and the interpretation of the standard Christian terms has been given, elsewhere.[1] In brief summary, the programme runs thus—that man attains the spiritually ideal life by possessing within himself no thought, no feeling, no living impulse which is not born moment by moment straight from God, God thus exercising a real spiritual parentage, a veritable Fatherhood toward man, and man thus possessing the actual life of God within himself—that, since man cannot come near enough to God for the establishment of a relationship so intimate as this, and being unable, consequently, to ensure that

[1] *The Philosophy of Christian Experience,* chaps. iv., vi., vii.

THE RELIGIOUS PROGRAMME 57

God's actual life shall at every moment be reproduced within him, God has in Jesus Christ sent His own life (not a mere revelation of what it is, nor a mere message about it) down to the human level, Christ becoming thus literally the Life-giver to man, having life in Himself as the Father has life in Himself—that man must so relate himself with the ever-present Christ as to obtain this God-life which Christ holds—and that faith, whereby this is done, is the actual movement of man's whole personality (not a mere mystical contemplation) to identify itself with, and to lose itself in the personality of Christ. And it has been stated, also,[1] that, inasmuch as this is the *ideal* spiritual condition, not perfectly realised in any one, and inasmuch as man does not perform that one unbroken act of faith, coextensive with his entire earthly term, which would make all other religious exercises superfluous by establishing a permanent oneness between Christ's life and his own, man must keep up a process of spiritual self-culture, inviting and welcoming freely all the worthy influences that seek to act upon him, and warding off the bad, till the perfect experience is attained. And if the religious programme be thus conceived, it is easy to see how an undertaking of the religious programme provides for a practical ordering of life

[1] *The Philosophy of Christian Experience,* chap. viii.

that shall be automatically right and true. In what the programme prescribes, both in regard to man's dealing with God and in regard to man's dealing with himself, it works straight toward the ultimate Christian ethical ideal.

I

If we regard the religious programme so far as it deals with man's ideal relationship with God, it becomes evident that the religious programme provides for an automatically right ordering of life on its practical side. For the programme, as just summarised, does not offer either a purely forensic or a purely mystical view of religion, and does not, therefore, stand disconnected from life's practical concerns, as does any religion to which either of these terms could justly be applied. That the view of religion offered in the Christian programme (if the brief summary of it given above be correct) is not merely forensic, it is hardly necessary to prove; for in that it speaks of the actual possession of God's own life by man, of a veritable spiritual parentage exercised moment by moment from God to man, of a line of spiritual heredity running ceaselessly between the two, it amply clears itself from any suspicion of looking upon the religious life as consisting simply in the acquisition by man of a legally blameless position and standing in God's sight. And it may at least be said—though much more remains to be said afterwards by way of positive affirmation—that the processes and experiences suggested by this language imply changes in man's inward condition by which outward conduct cannot fail to be in great measure turned upon worthy lines. Certainly the Christian programme cannot be said to be out of relation to life's practical concerns by reason of any legal fictions (such as may lurk, for instance, in certain mistaken interpretations of the doctrine of justification by faith) concerning the relations between God and man; and it is impossible to charge against it, on the ground of any "forensic" dealing with those relations, that a man may have religious experiences without being affected in the practical conduct of life. To be in union with God, in any real sense, must make a difference to man's ethical conceptions, and to the way in which he embodies them in word and deed.

It is, perhaps, not so immediately evident that the Christian programme of the religious life escapes the danger of falling into mysticism, and, as a consequence, dropping out of relation with practical concerns. Yet a little thought suffices to establish the fact. It is, as has been said, upon an actual sharing of the life of God Himself, upon the production of a real spiritual heredity running at every moment from God to man, that the

Christian programme concentrates; and it is by the identification of man's personality, through faith, with the life of God as brought near in the personality of Jesus Christ that this communion of life is brought about. It is true that surrender to God, rather than striving or knowing, comes thus to be the watchword of the saintly life. But whether or no this surrender, this concentration of one personality upon another, will have results which show themselves in the practical sphere, necessarily depends upon the personality to which man gives up his own. If that personality be itself ceaselessly working, ceaselessly seeking to realise itself and its purposes through every detail of the history of the world and of human life, then man's abandonment to that personality must mean, not that man's activities remain unaffected, but that they are heightened and intensified and turned upon the line of perfectness. In the idea of a higher personality seizing upon and dominating a lower is involved the idea of the higher personality's *activity* seizing upon and dominating the activity of the lower. And, since it is a ceaselessly working and active God whereof Christianity speaks, surrender to that God must imply that all the work and activity of surrendered man are made and held right and true. Surrender to a perfect and active God must bring with it a perfecting of man's practical programmes down to their minutest detail. Doubtless mysticism, as it has existed in the Christian Church, has frequently forgotten this; but the critics of mysticism have frequently forgotten it too. As man reaches the point of taking life from God instead of making his own, he takes the activities of God in substitution for activities of his own; and a real surrender to the divine life leads inevitably to a perfected morality and to an ethical programme which harmonises with and forms part of that eternal working carried on from the beginning by the energies of God.

Indeed, in its insistence on surrender, in its emphasising of the self-abandonment of man to God as the all-inclusive religious programme, in its usage of what might be called mystical speech, Christianity always assumes—always keeps, as it were, in the back of its mind—the idea of God as active, and thus guards itself against the risk of making a mere passive contemplation of the divine perfections the beginning and end of the Christian life. It sums up the necessary relationships which man must assume towards God as "knowing God," as "seeing Him as He is," as "loving Him" rather than as knowing Him in the purely intellectual sense, as having towards Him the receptive mind and heart of "a little child." In these and other ways it describes that movement of the human personality up to and into the divine personality by which a right relation between man and God is set up. But it is always the *whole* man moving out upon the *whole* God, the *whole* God moving down upon the *whole* man, that it contemplates—the activity of God thus supplanting the activity of man, as well as a God-ward emotionalism being kindled in man's heart and responded to from God's. In fact, in the New Testament saying, " We know that, if he shall be manifested, we shall be like him; for we shall see him even as he is," the secret of a perfect ethics, notwithstanding the ring of mysticism in the words, is given. The experience of our common life gives some illustration of the principle involved. In our companionships, we always tend to grow in character like to those on whom the inward vision broods, and, through our growing likeness of character to them, to assimilate our practice—almost unconsciously—to theirs. So soon as we are able to get to a contemplation of our friend's character, as distinguished from the mere outside and accidental circumstances which surround him— when, in other words, we see him *as he is*—the qualities of character in him begin to take a hold upon us and to reproduce themselves—inevitably reproducing, also, their practical consequences— in us: we cannot abandon ourselves to a real, continued, undisturbed "seeing" of another without, in measure proportioned to the intensity of our "seeing," having our nature and conduct conformed to his. Of course, one comes now and again upon instances of a mere mechanical imitation of one person by a second: some trick of manner, some habit of action, catches the imitator's fancy, and he adopts it as his own. It is not with this that we are concerned; for that mechanical imitation implies no real "vision" of character at all—though it might be remarked, in passing, that it fairly corresponds to a patching and alteration of outward conduct in order to bring it into correspondence with a divine pattern, without that previous "vision" of the divine personality out of which the perfect outward conduct should come. But the companionships which mould us, the friendships which really bring a change upon the moral make of us and upon the consequent practical ordering of our life, are those in which we permit the character of companion or friend to reveal itself to us, and in which, simply surrendering ourselves with calmness to that character's spell, we do nothing but "see." Because he to whom we thus submit ourselves is an active and working being, with impulses ceaselessly pressing out into practice, surrender means for us something more than an emotional impression—means a heightening or lowering of conduct to the level on which our friend maintains his own.

It is a similar process, but intensified by many degrees, that Christianity contemplates when it sets "seeing" God, abandonment to God, surrender of human life to God's life, in the forefront of its programme as the essential thing. It contemplates man as so stretching himself up and out toward God that God, returning upon man in *all* the qualities of His own life and character, shall make man's life—in its activities, necessarily, as well as in all else—only an adjunct of His own. A similar process, it has been said, but a similar process intensified by many degrees. For a really complete abandonment to the "seeing" of what another is, is never attained in human experience —a fact for which we may perhaps be thankful, since an exact reproduction of any character in this world would not mean the winning of perfection. Our vision of others is never more than partial; and our imitation of others, in temperament and activity, is therefore never more than partial either. But in our relationships with God, that entire abandonment to the seeing of what He is comes to be the one thing we need, since (He being what He is) the perfect vision of God, which would be the perfect transforming power for man, would make us, in character and conduct, to be complete. Holiness, seen as it is in

THE RELIGIOUS PROGRAMME 65

God, could not fail to get an absolute hold upon us; and, since holiness in God is active and working, our practical programmes would, under the influence of the "vision," be no longer ours, but God's, and consequent holy as God's own. The constant seeing of Him must draw from Him into us what His own perfectness holds—the perfection of His activity, among all other things. And when it is suggested that the Christian programme makes for a mysticism which has little or no relation to practical concerns, the reply is clear. It is a ceaselessly working and active God of whom Christianity speaks; and, in all its speech of most mystical ring, it contemplates the *whole* man moving out upon the *whole* God, and the *whole* God moving down upon the *whole* man.

One may claim, indeed, that those terms of the Christian programme which are possessed of mystical suggestion need to be, not put aside, but pressed home in their full significance, if one is to see how the Christian programme makes for ethical completeness. It may appear a strange thing to say; but the failure of mysticism, in so far as it has failed, has lain in the fact that it has not been mystical enough; and its critics, instead of assailing its principle, should have bidden it apply its own principle with greater stringency and force. The error of mysticism has been that it has taken surrender, contemplation, the " vision," too exclusively as an alternative to intellectual processes, as a method of knowledge to be substituted for the ordinary methods of mind and brain. And against a mysticism which so limits its own ideal and its own hope it may be plausibly contended that its bearing upon practice is only remote. But all the mystical terms of the Christian programme need to be pressed till they yield the conception of the *whole* man uniting with the *whole* God; and in such a union as that, having given up the intellect as the chief factor in the construction of his moral and spiritual religious life, finds that he gains much more than the intellect, even in its most successful enterprises, could ever have won. He gains a spiritual relation with God which touches upon, and expresses itself through, the condition of his entire character and the activities of all his outward life. He has accomplished, by the way of surrender, something that intellect could never even have *attempted* to do. The success of intellect would have been at its best only the accomplishment of the preliminaries to the success of the soul and the purification of conduct: this method of "vision," substituted for the processes of intellect, accomplishes the preliminaries and the ultimates in one. And the mystical language of Christianity is not understood until it is taken as pointing to a completed spiritual process like this; and in this complete understanding of it one realises that Christianity provides for the purification of conduct, not *in spite of,* but *because of,* the mystical element it contains. Mysticism, in short, must become yet more mystical if it is to be a practical force, and to correspond in its findings with the true Christian idea. It is true that the Christian programme makes no such unqualified depreciation of reason as mysticism has sometimes made. But mysticism has been led to make its unqualified depreciation of reason because it has looked upon the method of " abandonment " it advocates *simply* as a substitute for reason; and the sharpness of the antithesis in which it has allowed itself to be caught has compelled it to reject one element with something like scorn. The Christian programme holds that no time and labour spent in making our intellectual understanding of God as complete as possible are spent for nought. But it declares that, after all this is done, there remains a method of " abandonment " by means of which intellectual findings will be confirmed, and over and above that, spiritual and ethical results secured. For its method of abandonment means, not only the substitution of something else for the brain as the instrument of approach to God, but, once again, the *whole* man moving out upon the *whole* God, and the *whole* God moving down upon the *whole* man. And if it be said that the

Christian programme, ringing with mysticism as it is, is out of relation with practical life, one may answer boldly, "Not if it be interpreted *mystically enough.*" Mysticism must stretch its understanding of its own terms till their connotation corresponds with the connotation in which the Christian programme employs them. A union of the *whole* man with the *whole* God is what the Christian programme keeps in view; and, thus read, thus pushed to the final point of their significance, its mystical terms—wherein, indeed, its very heart is contained—carry an inevitable implication of that ethical perfectness which they are sometimes supposed to ignore.

II

In what the Christian programme prescribes as to man's dealing with God, therefore, it cannot legitimately be held open to any charge of being out of relation with practical concerns. It is not guilty either of a forensic or of an unpractically mystical conception of man's relationship to God. On the contrary, in its ideal view of that relationship it provides for a practical ordering of life that shall be automatically right and true.

In its *ideal* view of that relationship—but, inasmuch as the ideal relationship is not perfectly attained in ordinary human experience, a further question has to be faced. Because man does not achieve the perfect dealing with God, Christianity prescribes a certain dealing of man with himself— a temporary religious exercise, so to call it, which is to be followed until the day of the perfect Godward attitude shall dawn. Is it true of this, also, that it has a direct bearing upon the ethical ordering of life, that it has practical issues, that it leads by a straight road to a perfecting of life on its practical side? All the watchfulness and care, all the introspection, all the self-sacrifice, all the detailed commands which the Christian programme lays upon the man who cannot once and for all lose himself in God, and thus render superfluous every other religious movement—are there any ethical consequences from all these things?

What has to be remembered is, that the Christian programme, in this aspect of it, aims always at *a spiritual self-culture which shall bring man nearer to that ideal spiritual condition (of really sharing God's life) out of which a perfect practice is bound to emerge.* Every precept it puts forth contemplates obedience to that precept, not as an end in itself, but as a factor in the process whereby the Christian makes himself ready for, and comes nearer to, the ideal spiritual state. And every precept it puts forth, therefore, looks onward to practical consequences, however disconnected it may for the moment seem to be from practical concerns, inasmuch as the ideal spiritual condition it forwards implies a setting right of all the practical issues of life. It is not so much for its own sake as for the sake of the spiritual culture brought about through obedience to it, that each precept goes forth—that spiritual culture, in its turn, leading up to a final union of man's life with God, and that final union issuing in a substitution of God's activities for man's. To summarise it once more—out of the ideal spiritual condition a perfected practice must necessarily come: since the ideal spiritual condition is unattained, man has to go through a process of spiritual self-culture to hasten its attainment: every one of the Christian precepts in the common religious programme has, when it is obeyed, a reaction upon that process; and every one of the Christian precepts, consequently, let its immediate concern be what it may, makes for a perfected practice in the end.

It is necessary to emphasise this, for it is sometimes alleged that the Christian programme, in its call to man for sacrifice, in its requirement of scrupulousness concerning matters which may appear somewhat remote, in its insistence upon the need of certain thought and feeling—in that entire *subordinate* and *secondary* discipline, so to call it, which it bids man follow till the perfect surrender can be achieved—is but causing man to

THE RELIGIOUS PROGRAMME 71

spend his strength for nought. All these things are looked upon as though they constituted a set of merely arbitrary commands, imposed simply as a test of man's submissiveness and constancy, and leading to a profitless absorption in the Christian's own condition—the practical side of life suffering in quality as a result. The facts are far otherwise. It is quite true that excessive emphasis may be set upon any or all of these things, that they may be attended to from inadequate motives, and with inadequate conceptions of the larger spiritual results to which they are meant to lead. But that does not affect the principle. In all its prescriptions the Christian programme keeps in view, as was said, a process of spiritual culture whereby the attainment of the ideal spiritual condition, with its consequent ethical perfecting of life, shall be hastened on. And it never calls for a mere emotionalism that begins and ends in itself, for a merely arbitrary dealing with mind and heart, for a purposeless sacrifice whose virtue lies only in its own pain.

When, for example, it bids man take order with his inmost thoughts, care not only for that which is without, but for that which is within, it is not because it holds that kind of introspection to have any special virtue in itself that it issues its command. It bases the command upon the undeniable truth that even the momentary thought, coming and going, and thus apparently done with, may do something to establish a tendency in the nature it visits, and that, according to the rightness or wrongness of the tendency so established or confirmed, a soul may be helped or retarded in its progress toward the ideal union with God, and consequently, in its progress toward a perfectly ordered ethical life. The subtle currents of thought—the momentary stirrings of emotion—the attention wherewith for just an instant the mind listens to some suggestion which it can itself hardly identify, some suggestion casually flung in from a voice that chanced to be wafted by—the countless thousands of moods and tempers and dispositions whose visits to us appear to make no mark of which, after they are gone, we can say, "*This* is the trace they have left"—all these things, the Christian programme declares, count and tell in that spiritual culture which the Christian man must maintain. They make the man—the character and tendency in him—if they make nothing else. And the Christian programme insists on care and watchfulness about these things simply because the treatment of these things bears upon the achievement of the final spiritual and ethical idea.

Similarly, when the Christian programme bids the Christian man keep himself constantly on guard as he threads his way through the various circumstances of his life, look upon himself as one who moves in a hostile land where foes may be lying ambushed on every side, and remember that even beneath the appearance of innocence some possibilities of moral disaster may lurk, it is not because it esteems an attitude of aloofness or of opposition as desirable for its own sake that it calls for this attitude of suspicious vigilance. The call is based upon the truth that the question of man's positive moral and spiritual culture is in all things to be supreme, and never even for a moment to be dropped out of mind. It takes into account the fact that even situations which appear to be morally neutral and colourless may, when brought to the bar of an unsleeping spiritual judgment, look far other than they did before: many an angel who seemed at a first glance to be clothed in heaven's white the while he summoned us, may turn out, when we compel him to repeat his call in the presence of a divinely-kindled spiritual sensitiveness, to be but a tempting devil in disguise; and for that reason, if for no other, the Christian programme bids us bring all possibilities, innocent as they may appear, into the spiritual world, the spiritual resting-place, before we drop into their inviting arms. Baneful consequences may come upon the spiritual development going on within us from things that look at first as if they could affect that spiritual development not at all. This call, moreover, takes into account the fact that many elements of man's environment, while not specifically good or bad in themselves, may nevertheless have some moral and spiritual reaction upon man's life: often and often is man confronted by various solicitations and opportunities, coming upon him through his contact with the world outside, none of which may possess any distinctive moral quality at all, but which may yet tend, some of them to the growth and strengthening, and others of them to the check and weakening, of that spiritual development and tendency in him whereby he is being carried on to the realisation of the ultimate Christian ideal: it is one of the wonders of life that we may do something which is in itself harmless, and yet be ourselves the less spiritual for having done it, and may take some course which has no special virtue in it, and yet be spiritually confirmed thereby. And it is with these facts in view that the Christian programme calls for an attitude of ceaseless vigilance, not to say suspicion, on the Christian's part. The maintenance of such an attitude bears upon the achievement of the final spiritual and ethical ideal.

And once again, when the Christian programme calls for self-sacrifice, bids the rich man sell what he has and give to the poor (whether or no the particular command, given on a particular occasion in the ministry of Christ, is universally and permanently binding or not in similar cases, is not for the moment the question) it is still with a view to the furtherance of spiritual culture that the demand is put forth. It is not for the sake of sacrifice itself, but for the sake of the reaction from the sacrifice upon the spiritual tendencies of character, that sacrifice is inculcated. Indeed, the principle underlying the special command in the case alluded to is simply this —" Do that which your circumstances suggest as the direct method, *for you*, of making the spiritual development of your nature secure." The young man's riches might be the weight to sink him down from all that was good; but they might be, on the other hand, the means of letting holy graces sweep through his life, if he used them rightly: and he was to give himself to that particular method of developing spiritual quality which the circumstances of his life had opened to him. It is, indeed, only when this underlying principle of the demand for sacrifice is grasped that the universal pressure of the demand is perceived. So far are we from explaining it away when we thus pass from its outward form to its underlying and penetrating essence, that we make it impossible for anyone to escape its grasp. Sacrifice in this way becomes binding upon all, whether or no they own goods of which they might dispossess themselves for the poor's sake. Sacrifice, indeed, is called for, because that turning of life to spiritual account, which is the principle beneath the demand, simply means sacrifice—the greatest sacrifice of which human nature is capable. To live ever watchful for opportunities of spiritual culture and advantage, caring for life only as it affords such opportunities, anxious to turn all experiences and all circumstances into food for the inner life—that is to be in the world but not of it; and to be in the world but not of it is precisely the sacrifice required. When the Christian programme calls for sacrifice, it calls for something that all can offer, be they rich or poor, high or humble—the sacrifice of living only for the spiritual, of making all things spiritual by the consecration of the use to which they are put. The fact that it is in connection with wealth that sacrifice is most frequently alluded to, though natural enough (since wealth has the most patent and obvious means at its command of manifesting the spirit of sacrifice), must not blind us to the truth that the essence of the sacrifice required by the Christian programme lies, not in the mere giving up of something, but in the turning of life's ordinary circumstances, whatever they may be, to purposes of holy culture and spiritual advance. The Christian programme calls for sacrifice, because sacrifice, when its principle is rightly understood, bears directly upon the achievement of the final spiritual and ethical ideal.

We repeat, therefore, that the Christian programme—in the entire subordinate and secondary discipline which it bids man follow till the perfect surrender to God can be achieved—aims always at a spiritual self-culture which shall bring man nearer to that ideal spiritual condition whence a perfect practice is bound to issue. Every one of the Christian precepts makes for a perfected ethics in the end. And thus we have made the point which in the present chapter we set out to make, have seen how the religious programme of Christianity not only *demands,* but *creates,* an automatic right rectitude of practice, and how religious attainment and ethical completeness are not two things but one.

IV

THE CHRISTIAN CONSCIENCE

BUT we have really done more than this. We have made the transition to the ethical principle, the ethical method, for every day and for every problem of every day, and have reached a conception of the manner in which the Christian conscience, applied to all common and uncommon questions of conduct, ought to work. We are prepared, in other words, to pass from the *ultimate* ethical ideal to the ethical procedure which the Christian, in default of realising that ultimate ethical ideal, has for the time being to adopt. The ultimate Christian ethical ideal, as we have seen, takes man as not really concerned with ethical questions at all, but as putting himself into such a spiritual adjustment that ethical questions settle themselves: it views him as adopting an automatic right attitude to every circumstance, as maintaining an instinctive right bearing toward every problem of duty and every temptation to wrong. But, inasmuch as that condition of automatic ethical self-adjustment is not yet attained, what is the Christian man to do? How

THE CHRISTIAN CONSCIENCE

is he to guide himself among the practical issues of his life? To what standard and along what lines is his conscience to work? Just as Christianity provides what we have termed a secondary *religious* programme for the Christian disciple—a secondary programme for the disciple's spiritual self-culture and self-discipline which the disciple is to follow till his life is really one with God's—so we have somehow to provide for the Christian's observance a secondary *ethical* programme which shall guide him till the ultimate ethical ideal be won. How, as he proceeds toward the final goal, can the Christian man discover the true key to the many doors which he must pass through on the way? It is the answer to this inquiry we have now to seek. Or rather, we have to show that the answer to it has already been found.

I

The ultimate religious ideal and the ultimate ethical ideal, as we have seen, fulfil themselves together; for that seizing by the life of God upon the life of man, that dropping of the life of man into the life of God, whereof the ultimate religious ideal speaks, involves, necessarily, the supplanting of man's activity by God's own, and thus provides for that automatic adoption of right courses wherein the ultimate ethical attainment consists. And in the secondary religious programme, in the programme rendered needful by man's present failure to carry the ultimate programme through, the same close connection between the religious life and the ethical is, as we have also seen, still maintained; for through all the disciplines imposed by that secondary programme the realisation of the united religious and ethical ideals is steadily kept in view; and the process of that realisation—the fact that the Christian man is engaged in it—is looked on as regulative of the Christian man's attitude towards the world and towards all the circumstances of his common life. We have seen, in fact, looking at things from the religious point of view as distinct from the ethical, that we are nevertheless compelled to take the ethical also into the range of our vision. We have seen that, both at the highest stage of development and at the intermediate stages, the inner religious life and the outer practical life are, according to the Christian reading, in closest relationship—and in relationship constituted not merely by some bond of logical antecedence and sequence, not merely by some scheduled order of succession, but in a much more vital and organic way. It is, of course, at the loftiest stage of spiritual development—when (if it were only attained) spiritual life and ethical practice would be, so to say, like two suns which have at last come to lie exactly edge on edge, and have been fused into one—that this close relationship would be most perfectly discerned. But even at the lower and intermediate stages the Christian religious programme founds itself upon that same relationship, and, although compelled to admit that between the inner religious life and the outer practical life there is no such mutual permeation, fusion, interpenetration, as would be brought about by the perfecting of the first, insists, at least, upon the action and reaction of the two as a governmental fact. The Christian programme presents man as enwrapped in the spiritual development that is going on within him, as being ever conscious of its goal, as making that remembrance and that consciousness regulative of his dealing with all contingencies, and as then finding his spiritual development in its turn helped on toward the ever-beckoning goal by the reflex action of the practical concerns themselves. The progressive spiritual life is to manifest itself through, to dictate to, and to feed itself by, the ethical activities of each successive hour. The close relationship which is absolute fusion at its highest point, and which is to be ceaselessly anticipated under that aspect by the ceaselessly progressive soul, is at least to be maintained as action and reaction while the lower stages are passed through.

In common life, however, the Christian man has constantly to attack the matter from the other end; and it is from the fact that he has some ethical problem to grapple with immediately rather than from the fact that he is passing through a process of spiritual development whereto all things are to be subservient, that he is compelled to start. While the religious programme of Christianity views him primarily as a developing spiritual nature, as realising himself to be that, and as never reaching out upon the practical problems of this life except from his standpoint in that consciously apprehended development, the Christian man, as a matter of fact, does not thus at first see all things in the light of, and as related to, the spiritual process going on within. His consciousness of himself as a developing spiritual nature is not a constant thing: it is not always at home, so to say, to receive the ethical problem when it comes knocking at the door; and it is not as held within that consciousness, and as equipped by it for judging, that the Christian man unintermittently faces the practical questions of his days. According to the religious view, it is to a growing divine life in man, alertly and livingly conscious of itself and watchful of its interests, that ethical problems always present themselves. They are always the second thing to arrive; and they do but defile past while the regnant spirituality sits unmoved upon its throne. According to actual fact, the throne itself is frequently unoccupied when the ethical problems appear. Even the secondary programme of religion, as we have called it, does not so permanently grip the Christian man that he is always conscious of himself as carrying it through. And ethical questions, as one by one they appear, consequently involve a repeated reconstitution of the court in which they are to be tried.

Nevertheless it is in that ceaseless action and reaction between the inward life and the outward activity, whereon the religious programme insists —it is in this that we can find the secret of the Christian's bearing among the practical difficulties and problems of each successive day. If the consciousness of being engaged in a development of the divine life be not palpitating within, the revivification of that consciousness is the one thing needful when the ethical problem makes its appeal: if it be not at home when the practical question comes knocking, let it be at once fetched back. If the relation between the inward spiritual development and the outward activity be not, so far as its first term is concerned, antecedently prepared, let it be *made,* or rather *remade*, at the moment of the crisis. The Christian man must, as it were, work the formula backwards. The distinctly religious programme of things says, "Here is a nature wherein the development of the life of God through Christ has reached a definite point, and is going on toward the ultimate goal—and this developing life, conscious of itself and of its destiny, is to be brought into a relationship of action and reaction with outward activities and practical concerns." The Christian man, having failed to keep at its full height the consciousness of a developing divine life within, and not having made that consciousness *antecedently* as operative as it should have been, is to say when the ethical problem clamours, "Here are outward activities and practical concerns—and they are to be brought into a relationship of action and reaction with that inner process of a divine life's development wherein my nature is engaged." He must, in brief, before each new question on the side of *doing,* realise himself afresh on the side of *being,* become freshly conscious of himself as on the road to the ultimate spiritual ideal, and from that standpoint survey the new question he is called upon to face.

II

What this really means is that the divine life in the Christian, in its actuality and its potentiality, is to govern each ethical situation as it emerges into view and presents its appeal. It is not he, but God present in him through Christ, that is to deal with the successive problems of practical conduct, and to pronounce the decisive word at every crisis of life: it is not merely as a man specially endowed, but as a *Christian*—that is, as a man whose life is identified with, and in measure supplanted by, the life of God in Christ—that the Christian is to face the ethical questions of his days; and in this matter of ethical judging and decision, as in all other matters, the true line is given in the apostle's affirmation that it was not he, but Christ in him, that lived. When we say that the Christian man must, before each new question on the side of *doing,* realise himself afresh on the side of *being,* become freshly conscious of himself as on the road to the ultimate spiritual ideal, and from that standpoint survey the new question he is called upon to face, it is not meant simply that he is to recall the *idea* of the spiritual development wherein he is engaged. What is meant is that this spiritual development, the developing spiritual life, is *itself* to become regnant over the position. The Christian man is, at the hour of difficulty, to suspend his self-activity and to permit the Christ-activity to have the directive place which, as a matter of fact, it ought always to have, but from which the assertive self-hood of the Christian man too frequently keeps it away. It is the divine life in the Christian, in its actuality and its potentiality, that is to govern the ethical crisis as it comes. The divine life in its actuality; for the divine life is in measure already in possession of the Christian man, if he be at all worthy of the name. The divine life in its potentiality; for if the divine life be really present it will be stretching on within the Christian toward the fuller realisation of its own ideal, and will further that fuller realisation by every exercise of itself that it makes. The divine life is to deal with the practical problems, both expressing and developing itself by so doing—so establishing that relation of action and reaction whereof we spoke before. It must, indeed, develop itself in the very act of expressing itself; for, being actual life, it cannot fail to strengthen itself. As life always does strengthen itself, by each due performance of its functions. The point just now to be chiefly insisted upon, however, is that it is the actual divine life within the Christian that is to direct and rule. The Christian man is to become conscious of himself on the side of *being* when the practical question comes up,—yet it is not his *consciousness* of being something, but the *fact* of his being something, or rather it is that actual something itself, which is to be the operating and determining power. Nor is it by an effort of imagination that the Christian man equips himself for a grappling

THE CHRISTIAN CONSCIENCE 87

with the practical concerns. It is by an actual movement of his own life and of the Christ-life within him, a movement that swings each to its proper place. It is not a matter of imagination —or, if in any degree it be this, it is imagination that goes far to fulfil itself. The Christian man is to become freshly conscious of himself *as* a Christian man, and of what is implied therein as to his actual condition and as to his spiritual ideal: he is to realise himself as engaged in a process of developing identification with the divine life, and to anticipate, so far as is possible, what that process will lead to when it is complete; but, by the terms, the process anticipated or imagined as complete is already being actually carried on; and the Christian's very consciousness of what he is and of what he is to be, is really, if it be genuine, the divine life within him energising and bearing witness to itself. And so, once again, it is not the Christian's *consciousness* of the divine life—not his mere intellectual conviction that he is being made by the divine life— that is to be brought to bear upon the ethical problems: it is *the divine life itself* that is to deal with the problems and to decide. The Christian, confronted by the crisis, gets into the background where he should have been all the while, and calls upon the divine life within him to take its power and reign. He withdraws, to let the

Christ-life in him take sway. He realises himself —not in the mind only, but through all his nature—on the side of being, and thus transformed (not merely illuminated or strengthened, but transformed) goes out to meet the problem that waits. Or, instead of saying that the Christian man realises himself afresh on the side of being, one might put it that the Christ-life, which is in measure making him already, and which is pressing on in him to its fulness, realises itself afresh in him, and comes to its own. At any rate, it is the divine life in the Christian, actual and potential, that is to govern and master each ethical situation as it comes into view. It is the divine life in the Christian, both expressing and developing itself in its dealing with the position, that is at the hour of every new practical decision to be regnant and supreme.

To put the matter in this way is by no means to countenance a mere subjectivity in ethics, or to make the standard of conduct liable to constant variation at individual caprice. " In thus throwing the different ethical decisions entirely upon something *within* a man," it may be said, " instead of looking upon them as being rightly taken only when they result from a man's desire to conform himself to some outside rule or ideal, you are allowing every man to be a law unto himself, and thus bringing confusion into the whole

ethical scheme." By no means. For it must be
remembered that the conception here advocated is
that of the action of one constant power—the
divine life of God, through Christ, in possession
of the whole nature—within every Christian man.
Different as men may be, the power within them
is, according to the conception, always the same;
and this power, could it speak its word and have
its way unhindered, would necessarily, being
itself unchanged, come always to a uniform ethical decision and produce always a uniform ethical
result. As a matter of fact, the view which has
here been taken implies a deliverance from subjectivity, rather than an establishment of it; for it
is not the man, but the divine life (working *within* man, indeed, but yet *not* man) that is considered to be dealing with the practical problems of
life. Perfectly translated into experience, this
view would eliminate all differences of moral
judgment on the human side, inasmuch as every
human judgment would be but another instance
of the same divine life judging through all—and,
the judge being the same, the judgment must be
unvaried too. It is true that, at the present level
of human experience, Christian men may, according to their varying degrees of self-identification
with the divine life, arrive at varying interpretations of what that divine life in them declares. But an objection of similar order may be

taken to any system which relies upon some external standard of conduct. For under any given conditions men will differently conceive the necessary applications and requirements of that external standard: their individual temperament and mood and intellectual bias will colour their reading of the entire position, even though the ultimate testing principle lie quite separate from themselves; and it is impossible to escape altogether from the subjective element, even by the setting up of some objective rule. The view here taken provides, at any rate, as other views do not, for a *final* freedom from that subjectivity which, for the present, does not cease to intrude. The life of God, were men entirely in its possession and entirely identified therewith, would in all men have but one voice. Precisely because the view for which we have been contending looks to the taking of all ethical decisions by one constant thing within every man—by something which, although working within man, is yet not of man but of God—it can repel the charge of subjectivity, and can declare that, so far from establishing subjectivity, it has banished it from the moral field.

Nor, let it be briefly noted (although the point will be more clearly seen when we come to deal directly with the Christian's relations with his fellow-men), does this view make for any self-

THE CHRISTIAN CONSCIENCE

centred and individualistic conduct of life. It loses nothing, for example, that is possessed by any system wherein the law of love is proclaimed as the decisive factor. In saying that the divine life in the Christian man, both expressing and developing itself in its dealing with the position, is to govern each ethical situation as it comes into view, do we become too individualistic, leave insufficient scope for altruism, and remove man's relations with man too far from their rightful place in the moral scheme? Not so. For the "divine life" which is to become governmental is itself "love," since Love is one of God's loftiest names; and the divine life, expressing itself through its dealing with any ethical situation, cannot fail to express itself as love so far as the situation permits or requires, and, developing itself through its dealing with any ethical situation, cannot fail to make the man it is progressively mastering more loving still, so far as the situation gives scope so to do. To hold the actual divine life in man for the controlling and directive ethical power is to give full room to love—for God Himself is Love.

One other word remains to be said before we pass on. We have seen how the spiritual ideal, already partly realised, and continuously making progress toward a fuller self-realisation, is to govern the ethical ideals of every passing hour. We have seen in what way that close relation between the management of the inner life and the management of the outer—that relation which is absolute fusion at its highest point—is to be maintained as action and reaction while the lower stages of experience are passed through. That is, we have done what at the outset we saw was necessary to do. *We have related the ideals to the ideal.*

III

The function of conscience, in the Christian man, is to decide whether or not ethical problems are being dealt with in the indicated way—to give warning that this is the way in which they should be dealt with, and to reprove if any other way be adopted. In other words, the inner voice which for men outside the distinctively Christian rank declares that they must choose the path of right, becomes in distinctively Christian men a voice declaring that not they, but the divine life in them, must make the choice.[1]

Let it be remembered, in this connection, that even conscience (for the moment it is not the specially Christian conscience, but conscience in general, of which we speak) is not, strictly taken,

[1] For the completion of the statement concerning the function of conscience, see page 240.

an infallible guide to conduct—though it is often spoken of as if it were. Conscience, even at its very best, tells us whether we have selected, out of the various possible courses open to us, the one which we judged to be right: it does not assure us that the course we have judged to be right is really so. It is impulse and motive, not action itself, whereof conscience is judge. Through conscience a man knows whether or not he has been faithful to what his mind estimated as the higher of two alternatives; but whether the alternative he has estimated as the higher is, when judged by the absolute standard, the higher in truth, is another question altogether. In our ordinary speech we talk about conscience deciding between this and that, settling upon this method of life as being conformable to the law of goodness and rejecting that other method of life as being out of harmony with the requirements of that law; and in our ordinary speech, perhaps, this may be allowed to pass. We put together, so to say, the process of determining which method of life appears to be the right one, and the other process of self-approval or self-disapproval which goes on within us according to our obedience or disobedience to the indications of the first; and we speak of conscience as the faculty in us which performs them both. But, if we are to aim at exactitude of expression, we are compelled to declare that conscience does but acquit or condemn us as having adopted or spurned what our minds held to be right,—but that, whether the judgment of our minds as to what is right was a judgment accurate and true, a judgment which God, did we present it to Him, would confirm, it is not within the province of conscience to pronounce. Conscience is the voice within everlastingly reminding man that right is the one thing to be exalted above all else; it is not a voice explaining to man what right is. Let a man look into his conscience, and he will know whether, when he made his decision just now, he made it because he thought right commanded it, or because some meaner motive was allowed to have sway; and he will be at peace on that point if conscience applauds, ashamed if it look on him with a frown; he will *not* know whether, when he made his decision, he was not leaving out of his reckoning elements which should have entered in, and whose absence vitiates the decision at which he arrived. Conscience simply declares that what is judged to be right should at all costs be done.

For the Christian man, the verdict of his own mind as to what is right is to be supplanted, as we have seen, by the decision of the divine life in him. And conscience, still sitting as monitor and judge, judges now a different cause. It decides,

THE CHRISTIAN CONSCIENCE 95

not whether the man has followed his sense of right, but whether he has permitted the divine life in him to be the guiding power. Just as, for men outside the distinctively Christian rank, conscience judges actions, not in themselves, but in their relation to what is believed to be right; so, for the Christian man, conscience judges actions, not in themselves, but in their relation to the divine life which is progressively realising itself within—applauds or condemns the actions themselves according as it is or is not from the actual initiative of that divine life that they proceed. The terms of the inquiry whereto conscience furnishes the answer have, for a rightly ordered Christian experience, been changed. The inquiry is no longer, " Has the man done what he believed to be the right?" but " Is it the man himself, or the divine life in the man, God in him through Christ, by whom the thing has been done? Is it the progressive spiritual life in the man that is manifesting itself in, dictating to, and feeding itself by, the ethical activity of this particular hour?" And according to the " yea " or " nay " wherewith the Christianised conscience answers its own question does the Christian man, at each successive moral crisis of his life, stand vindicated or condemned.

It is for this message, then, as it issues from the inner voice, that the Christian man must listen if he would know what, from the Christian standpoint, the moral quality of his own acts is found to be. To the inward monitor which emphasises the necessity of substituting the decisions and the activity of the divine life within him for the decisions and the activity that spring from the self in him, he must ever give watchful and alert heed if he would save himself from reproach. It is quite true that the Christian man, living under the direction of his voice, will sometimes be brought, in the final issue, to the same outward deed as the man who, under ordinary operation of conscience, pursues what his judgment chooses as the true course; so that for the world at large, as it watches, there may be no clearly marked difference between the treatment accorded to the moral problem by the two. But the *spirit* of the two actions, correspondent as they may be in external features, will nevertheless be altogether different—a fact which even the world at large will not seldom be able to discern: it will be to two wholly irreconcilable schemes of living that the two actions, with all their outward similarities, belong; and, in any event, the fact that the different initiative principles produce ultimately the same result will be only, so to say, an accidental circumstance in the case. And on the other side, let it be remembered that the Christian man, listening to the pronouncements of this inner

THE CHRISTIAN CONSCIENCE 97

voice, may often, as he looks back on his treatment of a moral crisis, be obliged to pronounce it faulty, not because it was so in itself, but because it was not from the direct initiative of the divine life in him that it sprang. Action may be right in itself, and yet, from the Christian point of view, may lack the highest quality. If the Christian fails to deal with a problem of conduct, with a moral question, distinctly *as* a Christian—from the heart and shelter of his Christian experience, as one whose life is identified with and lost in the divine—then he has fallen below himself, and the inner voice will condemn. An action initiated in self, rather than in the life that is intended to supplant self, does not satisfy the requirements of the Christian conscience, even though against the action, as it stands upon the record, no charge may lie. Unless it was the progressive divine life within that manifested itself in, dictated to, and fed itself by, the action under review, the essential quality was not there. The mere accident that the wrong method led to a right result is not sufficient to ward off blame. And the Christian man, let it be repeated, must therefore give watchful and earnest heed to that inner voice which emphasises the necessity of letting the divine life within keep all initiative, take every decision, and perform every action as from itself, if he would save himself from reproach.

Conscience, for the distinctively Christian man, must be taken as a monitor declaring that not he, but the divine life in him, is to make the choice; and in that sense must it be heard and obeyed.

IV

It is not suggested that the Christian man, endeavouring to hear and to follow the dictates of this inner voice, must infallibly be right in all his dealings with the moral problems of his life. For however keen may be his realisation of the fact that only indirectly, and through his abandonment to the divine life in him, should he attack those problems, the actual self-abandonment he makes remains, even at his spiritually most intense moments, incomplete: it is still, to some extent, the man himself as man, not altogether the man as Christian, that determines the practical issues: the purely human initiative does not *wholly* give way to, nor does the purely human judgment *wholly* sink itself in, the other and higher. It was pointed out before that in the ordinary moral operations of men (leaving the distinctively Christian method out of account) there are two stages—the first stage being the declaration of conscience that right must be supreme, and the second stage being the mind's delivery of its considered verdict as to what, in any given situation, actually constitutes the right which is to rule. Even in current Christian experience a similar dualism is not transcended. The first stage is now the declaration of the Christianised conscience that not the man himself, but the divine life in him, is to deal with the case. The second stage, which *ought* to be the infallible dealing, on the part of the divine life, with the question at issue, becomes, as a matter of fact, a dealing with the question at issue, *partly* by the divine life whereto the Christian man is genuinely abandoned, and *partly* by the man as man—by his own judgment, his own natural estimates, his own balancing of pros and cons. There is still some scope allowed, or taken, for the action of that purely human consideration of matters which, according to the Christian theory, has died into the activity of the divine life. The assertive self-hood, even of the Christian man, wrests from that life which is not himself, but God in him, something of its prerogative, and reserves for human judgment something of the field whence human judgment should have retired. And, since in the Christian man, no less than in others, judgment may easily go astray, the Christian, at his present level, is not guaranteed against a mistaken choice.

It should be noted, however, that on this view of what obedience to the Christian conscience consists in, an *ultimate* infallibility of practice is provided for, and the Christian, if he does not attain it, is at least set upon the road thereto. For obviously a complete self-abandonment to the divine life within, an utter yielding of all decision and all initiative to its power, would secure that infallibility, since the divine life could do no wrong. Even a perfect obedience to conscience, outside the distinctively Christian method, offers no complete safeguard against error, inasmuch as, after conscience has made its proclamation of the supremacy of right, judgment has to take the matter up and decide wherein the right consists. As a matter of fact, history records many crimes committed by men zealous for right and eager to obey what they understood to be the conscience-call: it is a commonplace that the greater enlightenment of later ages has frequently condemned as evil not a few courses of action which, in the day when men adopted them, were held to be inspired by heaven. But in a perfect obedience to the Christianised conscience the perfect safeguard, unattainable else, would most assuredly be won; for under that initiative and activity of the life of God in man, to which the Christianised conscience declares all moral problems must be handed over, error could in no wise creep in. The divine life, fully constituting, fully re-constituting, the man, could do no wrong.

THE CHRISTIAN CONSCIENCE

It is by the adoption of the view we have been advocating, therefore, that swiftest progress will be accomplished towards an infallible dealing with all the ethical crises of human life: though not yet attained, that infallible dealing at least comes more and more clearly within the range of vision as we progressively conform ourselves to the bidding of conscience, as it *should* utter its message to the Christian nature; and all the limitations and mistakes of human judgment are little by little transcended, little by little become of no account, as fallible human judgment yields its place to the regnant energising of God and God's life within. A perfect ethical code, if not reached, is at least provided for as an ultimate when the Christian man rightly interprets the imperative of conscience, and begins to yield himself to its voice.

On similar lines, it is evident that under this interpretation of the voice of conscience, as it speaks in the Christian man, and by an endeavour to obey its dictates, the Christian reaches to a greater likelihood (greater in precise proportion to the measure of the obedience he renders) of being right in any ethical decision he may take. His abandonment to the life of God within him is not complete, and in so far as it is incomplete the *certainty* of rectitude is destroyed; but the abandonment is at least in part performed, and in so far as it is performed the *probability* of rectitude grows. There is at least a higher element of judgment introduced into the Christian man's dealing with any moral crisis; and he is more likely, *a priori*, to take the true path through all moral entanglements, inasmuch as the infallible Counsellor, while not having it all his own way, nevertheless does take a real share in the determination of the issue. One may go so far as to say that even the ordinary moral instincts of the Christian man will work more truly for being in contact with that divine power in which they ought to be entirely lost. In any case, the Christian man, in so far as he deserves the name, has within him something which, even with its partial rule and its hampered sovereignty, increases his chances of rightly managing his life and elevates him, other things being equal, to a position of superiority over those whose natural moral instinct is left to its work unassisted by any higher power.

This, of course, is on the presumption that, at the moment of crisis, he who claims to be Christian does call upon the divine life within him to take such part in the control of the crisis as his imperfect spiritual experience permits. The pity of it is, however, that so many Christian men, face to face with some ethical crisis, forget the power they have at their command, forget for the time being that they *are* Christian men, and address themselves to the task of estimate and judgment, not as Christians, but simply as men. They make no call upon the divine life within them: they rather stand aside from it while they deliberate and choose: they wilfully fling away their advantages, and reduce themselves, for the purpose of grappling with the crisis, to the level of all the rest. It is on their own judgment that they throw themselves back—their poor, dazed, halting judgment, which has not even in them completely shaken itself free from the influences that prevent it from acting faithfully, which even in them may be so greatly warped by other judgments round about it—their narrow, short-sighted judgment, peering with infinite difficulty just a little way into the darkness encompassing it, and seeing the shape and size of everything wrong. It is quite true, as has been previously admitted, and as will be emphasised again, that even in the Christian man judgment must in the last resort be called upon to do its part. But as far as the Christian judges at all, he only judges to any purpose as he realises that he ought not to judge. And it needs to be solemnly remembered that, so long as man acts on unaided judgment alone, the way that seems right may be the way of evil—and this is as true for the Christian man as for any other. And the Christian man, when he thus lets his moral deliberations begin and end in himself, takes a risk that is as needless as it is great, for, being a Christian, he has open to him better and safer lines on which to work. And as it has been said that the Christian man, using his possibilities, has the greater likelihood of being right in the moral decisions he takes, so must the correlative truth also be set down—that the Christian man, not using his possibilities, has the less excuse if he go astray. He cannot say that, having done what appeared to him to be right, he is entitled to go free from blame. He cannot make that claim until he has obtained for the problems of life and conduct all the light and all the inspiration that are to be won—and he has not done that unless he has called upon the divine life within him to act. In measure the same principle holds good for all men; and none can escape censure on the plea of having taken the seemingly right course so long as they despise the divine assistance in finding what the right course is. But for the Christian man the principle is of specially binding force; for he has the divine life within him, and his fault is all the greater if he allow it to remain latent, so to say, when the hour of moral decision arrives. "I did what seemed to be the right thing: surely I cannot be harshly dealt with, even if my decision was at fault." Yes, but the question must be carried a step further back before the Christian man is entitled to feel at his ease. This may have seemed the right thing; but there is the next question, *Ought* it to have seemed the right thing? *Would* it have seemed the right thing if all possible means had been taken to find out what the right thing is? And the Christian man cannot say that he is thus doing all that is possible to him for the true control of life on its practical side, cannot claim that he is using all the forces at his command, till, at each return of question and problem, he summons into action that divine life which, if his profession of Christianity be genuine, is at least in partial measure making him, and bids it master the crisis of the hour. The Christian man, if he would realise his own best possibilities and so save himself from blame, if he would understand conscience and obey it, must ceaselessly (and this not only in thought, but in practice) relate the ideals to the ideal.

V

CHRISTIAN DISTINCTIVENESS

AT our present point of view we are prepared to understand that, on its practical side, the Christian life will possess a special distinction of its own; and we are prepared to understand, also, why this must be so. The fact has already been insisted on;[1] and it has been stated that, even though the Christian system removes the main emphasis of thought from questions of conduct, or looks forward to such removal as the final thing, it is not because the Christian system holds conduct of small account. Christ was not going to have it supposed that the new preaching meant any lowering of the standard of practical life. It was, however, when we were looking at the *ultimate* Christian ethical ideal, and in connection therewith, that the point was previously made; and the special idea was that Christianity, while losing the moralist in the saint, stands for a higher standard of practice than the most rigid and stringent moralist could set up or reach. The idea immediately before us now is that the Chris-

[1] Chap. II. Sec. 2.

tian, even at the lower stages of his Christian development, ought to manifest a loftier conduct than is manifested by others, and should stand out in the world with a superiority of practice known and read of all.

The Christian ethical programme is, we have seen, that a veritable divine life, in part constituting the Christian, is to manifest itself in, dictate to, and feed itself upon, the practical questions which day by day arise. The Christian must, at the moment of crisis, allow the divine life within him to decide, and must, so far as is possible to him, withdraw all initiative of his own into the background, letting that divine life rise to fuller flood than it normally attains. He is to put himself by an effort which is only in measure an effort of imagination, and which, so far as it is that, is an imagination largely fulfilling itself into the position which he would occupy if the divine life made him wholly instead of only making him in part. But this—taking the moral and customary degree of the Christian's surrender to the divine life, and adding thereto the greater power which in the hour of crisis the divine life will, through the Christian's newly-accentuated surrender, obtain—this means that the practical questions of the Christian's life, the practical lines whereupon he moves, are in large part governed at the direct initiative of God Himself. The Christian should show a distinctive ethical product, for he is submitted to, and in part made by, a force which must surely bring about a distinctive ethical result. The divine life, working in the Christian, must surely do what no other force could hope to do. The Christian, if he be genuinely Christian, will in the nature of things prove himself to be at advantage in regard to the ethical standard he attains. As we remember that the Christian man is constituted by an altogether special *life-force* out of which all his ethical achievement should issue, we are on the one hand able to claim a special ethical possibility for the Christian man, and on the other hand obliged to warn him that, unless that special ethical possibility be at least in part fulfilled, he is not true to the name he bears.

I

In other words, if the doctrine of the Christian religion be true, there ought to be an altogether special quality in those who profess to hold it and to live by it; and the world has a right to look for something far above the average in those who claim to be its devotees. A profession of Christianity does not justify itself so long as the Christian is merely made and kept a good average man by his professed faith.

It is obvious that the larger the claims made by

CHRISTIAN DISTINCTIVENESS

anything—by any person or by any system of thought or religion—so much the larger must be the effects it produces, if the claim is to be allowed as valid. If any one claims simply to make some more or less helpful suggestions for the conduct of life—suggestions which, if carried out, will on the whole tend to elevate life and make it a sweeter thing, but suggestions which may admittedly fail in many cases and about which there is a certain amount of chance—well, in face of such a moderate claim we do not pitch our expectations too high, and he who makes the claim is not seriously discredited nor put to shame when nothing very much results. We say, "There was a certain margin of possible failure allowed for; and the smallness of the result is not matter for surprise." But no such "extenuating circumstances" are available if a professed Christianity fails to produce a special ethical quality in those who profess it. For the claim to be a Christian is really a claim to be dominated by the force of the divine life. Christianity does not speak in halting tones about what it can do: it does not simply say that, if all the conditions be favourable, and the life which tries it be of the right sort, it may be able to do something for that life and to make something out of it: it puts forward a claim that is universal in its reach. It declares itself to be both a necessity and a sufficiency, not for a percentage of the race, but for all its members; and it offers with confidence, not to patch up life in some degree, to give, as it were, crutches to the morally lame so that they shall be able to get on a little further, but to redeem life into a realisation of its most exalted possibilities; and it professes to contain within itself, because its method of action is what it is, the answer to every question that can arise in the management of the most difficult problems of practical experience. And the Christian, in declaring himself a Christian, declares himself submitted, at any rate partially submitted, to a power whereof all this can be truly said. Surely something special ought to come out of it all! This life-force which Christianity claims to bring—this life-force to which Christ's disciples say they have yielded themselves—does this wholly exceptional force produce no wholly exceptional effect? Can such a special power, brought to bear upon life, leave life unaltered in its main aspects and its main contents and its main issues? Or can such a special power, brought to bear upon life, do only what other powers could have done? One is shut up to the conclusion that there must be something wrong, either with the claim of Christianity or with the Christian's submission to it, if the Christian type of life does not pass beyond the moral average and reveal a quality all its own. For a veritable Christian distinctiveness we are surely entitled to call.

It is in the light of this consideration that the Christian needs to test his own moral achievement. If he be contentedly resting in the fact that he is not worse than the average, he has not realised what his responsibilities really are—the responsibilities laid upon him by his claim to be submitted to, made by, a divine life which must surely, in the practical effects it produces, leave the moral average far behind. If he be not ceaselessly holding up before the eyes of men a product, a manufacture of practical material, so to say, which shows that some altogether special spiritual forces have been at work, the worth of his Christian profession can scarcely be ranked as high. One ought to feel, as one passes within the Christian boundaries, that here one is in company with an altogether different make of man. If it be true, as is sometimes said, that the Christian disciple, taken on the whole, is simply a fair average man, then the position is nothing less than a satire on his profession of faith in Christianity and in Christ.

II

One needs to emphasise the further point that the distinctiveness of the Christian man is to be of a more than merely negative character. The pressure of the active divine life within him, out of which, by the theory, all his outward doings are to come, must result in a real and positive moral achievement, not simply in the avoidance of what is wrong. It is not by carrying further than others his abstinence from evil, but by a real manufacture of something distinctively good, that the Christian man fulfils the requirements of the case.

The point needs emphasising; for it is with the colourless life, the life about which there is nothing very particular to be said either in the way of good or of evil, that so many are apt to be content. The neutral life, the unpronounced life, the life which gets nowhere near the extremes of either righteousness or sin, but keeps a middle course deserving hardly any word of commendation or of blame, is perhaps the life most ordinarily found even in the Christian ranks. Men are satisfied—not to say proud—if they can but declare that they have kept clear of flagrant and open transgression, if they can take up this commandment and say, "Yes, that has not been broken," and turn to the other and say, "As to that, there is no charge against us," and thus, as to the actual commission of what is wrong, can claim to be acquitted of all blame. There may have been no special moral richness revealed in them, no very distinct revelation of holiness given in what they have said and done—but then there has not been, either, any special trace of positive sinfulness in the words they have uttered and the deeds they have wrought. They are content if upon the course of their existence the colours neither of good nor of evil are blazoned forth, if upon the whole of it they can preserve the one dull, neutral hue. And, indeed, such a life is always able to make out a good case for itself. The elder brother, standing beside the prodigal, and able to say with at any rate a large measure of truth, " I never transgressed a commandment of thine," appears entitled to feel something of satisfaction with his record. In a world where the enticements to wrong are spread out with an alluring fairness, where the prizes to be won by those who will turn aside from the path of outward rectitude are numerous and inviting, where forbidden practices and doubtful methods of living are tricked out with false beauties till the eye may be quickly deceived by their glamour—in such a world it is surely no small matter if we can proclaim ourselves to have no staring blots upon our robes! It may not be the highest thing; but it is surely a great deal!

Yet, if the method of Christian ethics has been truly set forth, all this really means very little after all. If the Christian is really in any degree made out of, constituted by, a veritable divine life, it is a very positive, and not a simply negative, virtue that he ought to show; for the divine life must have larger possibilities within it than those of mere restraint. And, as a matter of fact, one has only to look for a moment at the world's reading of things so far as life in general is concerned, to realise that in investing abstinence from wrong with so great an importance, we are treating the moral side of our life differently from all the rest. In all other things we recognise that only by positive progress and achievement does life become worthy; it is not when we can say that we have just kept clear of failure, but when we can claim to have overcome obstacles and won our way in their despite, that our voices have any proud ring of triumph in them; unworthy of our manhood should we think it if, day after day and year after year, we could but say that we have managed to scrape through. The rough wisdom of the world shows what it thinks of the man who is satisfied with mere avoidance of defeat when it declares that he who never makes a mistake will never make anything; and, although the saying may need to be somewhat qualified and toned down, it nevertheless contains a truth not to be despised. At any rate, it is in striving and in pursuit and in beating back of oppositions and in victorious achievement of most positive order that worthy living consists; and in everything else than the moral sphere, we all acknowledge that the case is so. It is by the amount of forward movement he can show us that we rank a man: it is as we can see that he forgot the things behind and pressed on to things before that we count him deserving of exalted place in the scale of manhood; and in all things it is by its eagerness and its upward straining and its determination to advance that human life wins aught of praise.

Is manhood, with a veritable divine life infused into it and in part recreating it, to be less forceful, less positive, than unassisted manhood feels constrained to be? In the sphere of practical life the transformed manhood of the Christian must, in all reasonableness, produce a result possessing a positive distinctiveness of its own. How can he be meanly satisfied if he does nothing that is particularly worthy of blame? Is this all that the pressure and operation of a divine life can do? Has that divine life no stronger initiative, no more forceful push? The effect bears no proportion to the cause, is utterly inadequate thereto. By his very profession of submission to the Christ-force, by his very claiming of the Christian name, the Christian takes upon himself the responsibility of positive production in the moral sense, inasmuch as such a positive production must inevitably result from any working of the force to which he yields. It is, indeed, only by an imperfection of submission, or by actual resistance—an imperfection and a resistance rendered more culpable by the partial acknowledgment made—that the Christian remains at the purely negative stage; and it is not too much to say that his very contentment with the absence of outward sinfulness is itself a sin. The blame of unresponsiveness falls with heavier weight upon those who profess to have responded in part. They have, so to say, given their case away. The Christian, if he have any title to the name, is in measure constituted out of the life of God, coming to him through his fellowship with Christ; and because that life cannot be conceived as any other than a forceful, initiating power, ceaselessly *making* its own special moral products and launching them upon the world through the channel of the human personalities it rules, the Christian life must ever manifest a positive distinctiveness of good. It is only in the nature of things that, if a professed Christianity be real, such a manifestation should be made; and the demand for it is but a demand that the Christian shall let the divine life in him work itself out and have its unhindered way.

III

Let it be remembered, also, that the Christian distinctiveness with which we are just now concerned is a distinctiveness of a practical kind. This is the counterbalancing truth to the truth previously insisted on[1]—the truth that in the construction of its ethical system Christianity begins by taking the emphasis away from conduct and setting it elsewhere. That is of primary importance; and yet Christianity only does that in order to find a means of elevating conduct to far higher levels. The very process of removing the primary interest from conduct, if the process be rightly carried through, results in a transformation of life on its practical side. It is for a *practical* distinctiveness in the Christian that we are entitled to look. One of the test questions is this, "How, in regard to the practical virtues—those practical virtues which some people, absorbed in religious enthusiasms and religious contemplations and those things which they dignify with the name of their inner religious experiences, are sometimes apt to forget all about —how, in regard to practical virtues, does Christianity work itself out in our case?" It is quite true that the Christian religion applies itself first of all, not to man's outward conduct, but to man's heart. It is quite true that it aims at transform-

[1] Chap. II. Sec. 1.

ing outward conduct, not directly, but by transforming inward character first. But it is also true that inward character cannot be transformed without issuing in a transformation of outward conduct, and in an excellence of practice beyond what was known before. And Christ Himself, in putting aside as touched with something of absurdity the idea that those who called themselves His disciples should *do* no more than others,[1] showed that it was thus He read the case.

The Sermon on the Mount, indeed, stands forth as supplying a tangible test whereby to some extent the practical achievements of the Christian man may be gauged. It is possible, of course, to take the Sermon on the Mount as the whole of Christianity—which it is not—and insistence on its ethical precepts to fall into the very error against which Christ was always warning His hearers, the error of fixing all interest and anxiety upon externals alone. Not that even the Sermon on the Mount does not call for much more than an outward righteousness; but ethics, as distinct from religion, bulks so largely in its contents that thought is apt to fasten upon the ethics and to forget the rest. The danger of falling into the indicated error is, however, avoided if we take a proper grasp upon the circumstances under which the discourse was

[1] Matt. v. 47.

CHRISTIAN DISTINCTIVENESS 119

preached. Probably the customary idea that it was delivered to a promiscuous crowd can scarcely be maintained; and the idea seems, indeed, to be negatived by the words in which the evangelist tells the tale. "And seeing the multitudes, he went up into the mountain"—with the purpose, clearly, of getting away from the multitudes—"and when he had sat down, his disciples came unto him: and he opened his mouth and taught them"—taught *them,* not the multitudes. It was to those who were actually in some measure disciples of Christ that the discourse was addressed. This does not mean that only the little band of men whom we call the Apostles heard Christ's words, but that He spoke to those who had passed beyond the stage of mere curiosity about Him, and who, however dimly and imperfectly, were really attaching themselves in some sort of personal relationship to Him. The discourse recorded in the sixth chapter of Luke—a discourse which on the surface bears the resemblance to a part of this—is probably a different one, addressed to the crowd as a whole. It is not so profound, not so spiritual, if the phrase may be employed, as the one that Matthew sets down. Some degree of true discipleship is pre-supposed in those to whom these words are given. And if this be borne in mind, there is no danger that even the closest student of the Sermon on the Mount will take Christ simply as a great moral Teacher, and nothing more. This ethical instruction which Christ was giving does but show how, on the practical side, discipleship is to work itself out. A real surrender to Christ, made in the way which in other sayings He prescribes, is pre-supposed before the ethical teaching begins.

But this said, we may repeat that the Sermon on the Mount stands forth as supplying a tangible test for the ethical achievement of the Christian man, and as affording indisputable proof that it is in practical virtue Christian distinctiveness ought to be shown. It is always useful to have a clearly marked standard to which we can refer: to estimate ourselves against a definite test scatters our delusions and breaks up our self-conceit and drives us to note flaws to which we have hitherto shut our eyes; and while it is undoubtedly possible to go through an ethical stock-taking too often, it is possible, also, not to go through it often enough. The Sermon on the Mount sets the standard, supplies the test, enables us to take stock of our moral properties. The Christian man must sometimes, if the apparent paradox may be pardoned, come back to the contemplation of his own external practice, and to a testing of it, in order to see whether he has in the first instance removed his care from his own external practice

CHRISTIAN DISTINCTIVENESS 121

in the right way. And, though the Sermon on the Mount does not cover all the ground of life—although, indeed, it is not by any self-conforming, either to the precepts of the Sermon on the Mount or to any others, that life is to be rightly ordered —yet the Christian may find therein the test whereby the spiritual processes he claims to have gone through can be judged. It is in a practical distinctiveness such as that discourse inculcates that a true Christianity must issue in the end. That practical distinctiveness is not the thing which the Christian sets himself directly to achieve—yet, if he be a Christian indeed, it cannot fail to emerge.

We are not concerned, in thus calling for a distinctiveness of Christian practice, with the controversy as to whether New Testament conceptions of virtue and duty are superior to all others the world has seen. However that question may be decided for each individual investigator's mind, it may for our present purpose be left on one side. They dispute sometimes whether Christianity brought in any originality of moral ideals—whether it revealed any new virtues, established any new conception of practical goodness before the eyes of men. An open-minded reader will most likely conclude as a matter of fact, that Christ at any rate claimed to have set up new standards of goodness, since He so emphatically contrasted His own "But I say unto you" with what had been said by the men of the older time. But, putting it as strongly as possible the other way, the call for Christian distinctiveness still rings clear. We may admit that, quite apart from religion and Christianity, there is a steady progress in the moral ideals of men, and that it is impossible to set any limits to its advance. But this remains—and it is on this that the call for a practical distinctiveness in the Christian is based—that Christ brought his disciples a power which will enable them to make fuller practice of the old good, *and that He expects them to use the power He brings.* Without Christ, men may know a great deal about love and generosity and all the rest: with Christ, they are to be carried far and far on into the practice of these things, finding in Him and drawing from Him that which enables them to do more than others have done. We come back again to the point that a divine life, manifesting itself through the Christian, must accomplish more than any other power can do. In regard to the practical virtues must the Christian disciple have something extra to show. The Christian disciple must be actually and measurably more kind, and more loving, and more forgiving, and more generous, and more truthful, and more morally courageous, and more all else that could be put into a catalogue of the graces than others are; *for he is submitted, according to his profession, to a force which must assuredly make him so.*

IV

Yet, to complete the thought, it must be added that it is on the common field, primarily and in the first instance, that this Christian distinctiveness is to be shown. Here, again, we base ourselves upon the underlying conception of Christian activity as issuing out of a veritable divine life; and we are entitled to declare that a divine life will find in the ordinary spheres and in the common relations of life ample scope for manifesting how special and unique a force it is. The very highest quality of Christian distinctiveness may be revealed without travelling out of the beaten tracks along which the mass of men wend their way. And when it is said that the Christian is to be marked off from others by a practical distinctiveness of his own, it is not so much meant that he is to take up a special programme as that he is to perform the old tasks in special ways and with special grace.

The average man (the average religious man included) would appear to cherish the idea that Christian distinctiveness—what is commonly termed saintliness—is, and must ever be, a thing entirely divorced from common experience. The very word suggests something wholly out of relation with the ordinary life of every day. The ordinary man may be religious, but a saint he cannot be: it is as though there were considered to be two brands of religion—a superior, to be manifested by certain elect souls alone, and an inferior, with which the crowds must be content: saints there have been and may still be, but they can hardly be looked for in the workshop or on the mart. And what lies beneath this idea is a feeling that Christian distinctiveness, if it be present, must prove and manifest itself through a special set of exercises which ordinary men find no opportunity of performing—that saintliness is, as it were, a separate profession or occupation in which ordinary men have no time to engage. They who would be spiritually distinguished, who would reveal the loftiest type of Christian activity, must forsake life's usual route and strike out for themselves a line far from the common paths. The feeling shows itself in many ways. The asceticism of the older centuries—the occasional recrudescence to-day of fevered denunciations of wealth and position as being things which must necessarily be sacrificed if spiritual ideals are to have their way—the demand, sometimes heard, that they who would be perfect must reduce their connections with the external world to a minimum, and put as great a distance between themselves and the common life as may be—are all signs of the idea that the highest character must manifest itself, not upon the usual stages of activity, but by distinct operations of its own.

Against mistaken ideas such as these, it needs to be declared that the essential proof and exercise of Christian distinctiveness consists, not in doing new things, but in doing the old things, the common things, in a spirit and fashion uncommon and new. And if at the first blush this appear a somewhat attenuated programme, unworthy of the dignity of sainthood, the true greatness of it —the reality of the change it implies for the whole of life—becomes clear with a little thought. It is a matter of common knowledge that two men may do each the same thing, and yet do it in ways totally different, so that under the manipulation of the finer mind the old thing becomes new. An ordinary routine may be, in a hundred subtle ways, lifted into something of greatness and touched with something of beauty, when it is taken in hand by a man of special quality. He may do nothing fresh, and yet the whole thing will take on a fresh colour and aspect from what he is. One man goes through the common programme as being common himself, as if at home with commonness: another, possessing some subtle quality within, makes the common programme great. Words convey a different shade of meaning on different voices: the same movement wears a varying significance according to the spirit that prompts it. It is quite possible for two lives, twin in all external things, to be worlds and worlds apart. And true Christian distinctiveness affords a more marked example of the same principle. The higher degrees of Christian attainment will find ample scope to reveal their presence and to exert their influence, even though the hands be kept to their old line of activity, and the feet stay in the old ways, and the voice speak on the old topics still. The divine life, constituting the Christian man, will necessarily mix some fresh ingredient of grace into that which grace had left almost uncoloured before. Even when no special opportunity comes in sight, and the worker has but his ordinary materials and his ordinary tools, it will, by some magic of its own, impart a touch of the special to that which has nothing special in itself. The man of Christian distinctiveness needs to be no exile from the homelands of ordinary men: he moves among his fellows with open eyes and ready steps, sharing their interests and one with them in many a word and deed; and yet, because he carries within him something that is peculiarly his, he makes old things new. True Christian distinctiveness is not something to *take the place of* common life, but something that is to dart through, and to make incandescence upon, the common life, as the electric current darts through, and makes incandescence upon, the wire.

In one way, perhaps the demand for a special quality manifested upon the old levels is a harder demand to meet than one for an altogether exceptional service would be. We are always far readier to undertake some special enterprise than to carry special quality into the old enterprises and bend it to the carrying out of the old call. The Christian disciple must bow himself to the demand, none the less. If the divine life be making him, it is to find room upon the old stage. He will not need to break away upon a fresh line in order that the new impulses governing him shall show clear. This is a case, it may be said, in which it is right to put the new wine into the old bottles. And each one must make the application for himself. Citizen, business man, politician—whatever any one may be—to show the excellence of discipleship, its distinctive quality, does not mean that these lines of life and activity need be left, or even in smallest degree slightingly esteemed, but that they are to be taken as the field, the platform, the sphere, in which the Christian, re-constituted as he claims to be by a life not his own, is to show how he can out-distance all the rest. And one could not, in all reasonableness, wish for a nobler mission than to reveal

—on the old stage where so many work without the propulsion of that inward life-force which we say is making us—what a Christ-inspired heart and a Christ-taught head and a Christ-directed hand can do. Through being possessed and made by a divine life, the Christian will show a distinctiveness clear to the gaze of all; but it is his first business to show it by taking the uncommon quality back into the world's common ways.

VI

THE CHRISTIAN'S RELATION TO THE WORLD

SO far, it is with general principles that we have dealt. Or, we may say that it is with the underlying motive power of Christian ethics, with the inner condition and movement and impulse out of which Christian ethics ought to be born, that we have been concerned. But amid the ordinary practical problems of life the Christian man will find that some further word of counsel is needed, in order that he may be fully equipped. And what remains to be said concerning the Christian ethical method can best be said in connection with some of those ethical problems which confront the Christian at almost every hour of every day. We may deal simultaneously (for a reason which will immediately become clear) with the question as to how the general principles already enunciated would work out in practice, and the other question as to how the Christian man, in the absence of their perfect working out, is to order his ways. For the two answers are really one. We pass now, therefore, to a more direct consideration of some of the spheres wherein the general ethical principles of Christianity have to be applied, some of the particular practical departments in which questions of Christian conduct are likely to arise.

The necessity for doing this arises from the fact, which has been repeatedly stated or implied, that the Christian man must in the last resort attack ethical problems, at any rate in measure, for himself. Theoretically, the Christian ethical system looks to an automatic settlement of practical matters through the government of the divine life within the Christian man; and the Christian man, at each emergence of the ethical crisis, has first of all to set himself in such an inward attitude that the divine life within him shall win increase of power, and take at any rate a large part in the settlement reached—the Christian conscience bearing witness whether or no this is done. It was previously said that something more than the *idea* of the spiritual development in which the Christian is engaged is to come into play as each practical crisis arrives: it is the *fact* of it— the developing divine life itself—that is to rule and decide. But the process of self-immersion in the divine life, carried to its utmost possible point at any critical hour, is not complete, and leaves still something for man to do. Since, abandoning himself as he can do by the sway of those impulses which are not his own, but God's, the Christian man nevertheless retains something of his ethical affairs in his own hands (in despite, as it were, of his own better will) he has to ask how, in any given case, this remnant of self-activity is to be ruled. The primary answer, of course, is, in view of all that has been previously said, that he must act as the divine life within him would act if it had all its rights. As was said in a previous chapter, the Christian, in so far as he judges ethical questions, judges them rightly by remembering that he ought not to judge. Properly speaking, ethical questions are to be solved by permitting the divine Personality, with which the Christian seeks perfect union, to attack them, rather than by any attack of his own: yet too large a margin of his own personality, so to say, remains outside the surrender at present accomplished, for this to be a true account of what is done. Obviously, therefore, that part of the Christian's own activity which remains working on its own account comes most nearly into line with the general ideal by regulating itself according to what the divine life would do (so far as this is ascertainable) if it had things to itself. The *idea* of spiritual development must be called on after all, since the spiritual development itself has not absorbed all regulative and directive power. Hence it is that the two questions previously referred to—the question as to how the general principles of the preceding chapters would work out in practice, and the other question as to how the Christian, failing their perfect working out, is to order his ways—really come to be one. And it must be remembered all through that the *idea* of the divine life is capable of exercising a right regulative power only when the *fact* of it is at any rate in measure a real and present thing. The Christian man has to remember that, according to the proper ordering of things, the divine life in him is to manifest itself through, dictate to, and feed itself upon, the activities of every hour; and in his own ordering of things, so far as any remains to him, *he must act as if this, and only this, were being done*. It is as a question of spiritual biology that every ethical question will come before his mind.

But this primary answer, thus given, at once raises a further inquiry. How, in the different departments of life, will this principle work out? The Christian man may legitimately ask to have the indicated method shown to him worked out in at least one or two examples, so that he may in other cases have some guide as to its use. We begin with the question of the Christian's relation to the world.

I

(*A*) THE CHRISTIAN AND MATERIAL GOOD

The first aspect under which the question presents itself regards the Christian's attitude to material interests and to material gain. How is the Christian man to bear himself so far as concerns matters of acquisition, increase of riches, and all the other things that come under the head of material good? Obviously, it must be recognised that there is a certain inconsistency, even a certain antagonism, between interests of a spiritual and interests of a material order. This is of course a commonplace; and theoretically the recognition has always been made. But it may be claimed that for the Christian who seeks to live by the formula enunciated—the formula that the divine life in him is to manifest itself through, dictate to, and feed itself upon, all the activities of every hour—and who makes that formula regulative of his ethical programmes, all the accepted precepts concerning his relations with the material world will stand upon a different and a definite basis. They will no longer be arbitrary enactments: they will not even be enactments in justification of whose promulgation certain more or less vague considerations of spiritual advantage may be pleaded: they will be realised as organically bound up with, as actually involved and implied in, the spiritual process which constitutes the Christian's life. They will be discerned as being, for the Christian man, inherent in the very nature of things, and will justify themselves so. The ideals will be related to the ideal. The Christian man, ordering himself in the suggested way, may in many cases (not only in the matter now in hand, but in many other matters) arrive ultimately at the same conclusion regarding duty as does the man who sets up some different standard—yet for the former the whole thing will be rationalised, unified, and in consequence the entire spirit of it changed. The commonplace that between the spiritual and the material a certain antagonism exists becomes more luminous, because more inevitable, for him who realises that the divine life within him ought to manifest itself through, dictate to, and feed itself upon, all his relations with the material world.

For it is only by strict subordination of the material that the process indicated in the formula can be maintained; and every one who has studied human nature, whether in himself or in others, will admit that between the lower and the higher there must always be war. The divine life in man, so far as it has been present, has always recognised this as a primary and undeniable fact. It stands out clear in the story of man's experience that for the loftiest spiritual results—in order that the divine life may first of all express itself, and then develop itself, in ceaseless rhythm —there must be a turning away as well as a turning to, a choosing which repudiates the lower as well as allows the higher to have a voice. Quite apart from the rightness or wrongness of any particular contact with any particular material interest, the Christian has to realise that the life within flourishes as the life connected with the material declines. The matter is not summed up for him even in the statement that interest in the material draws away interest from the spiritual. This ethical question of the Christian's attitude to the material becomes (as, indeed, do all ethical questions when treated on the indicated lines) a question of spiritual biology, to use the phrase previously employed. The Christian man has to reckon with the fact that the spirituality he possesses will not manifest itself, that fuller spirituality does not come within the prospect, except by conscious and deliberate discrimination between the interests of the outward life and the interests of the life within, and a conscious determination to make the interests of the life within supreme. The divine life within, did it have the entire control of the life without in its own charge, would make the discrimination. That we know. The Christian man, therefore, must make it for himself. He must realise how in the nature of things there is, between the inner and the outer, a great gulf fixed. And it is only as he realises this that the outer and material world subserves his spiritual welfare—that world's very irreconcilability, once accepted, making spiritual development more alert and intense. It is by making its relations with material interests to a great extent hostile, or at any rate by tinging them with aloofness, that the divine life in the Christian makes those relations assist its growth.

It is from this standpoint that we see the force of many of the utterances wherein Christ touches upon the relations between the spiritual welfare and the material welfare of man. For instance, the saying, "He that findeth his life shall lose it," obtains added significance when we set it side by side with the idea that the divine life within the Christian man is both to show itself in, and to develop itself through, the Christian's relation with the material world. The saying is perceived, indeed, to hold the same idea in other form. The Christian's ethical formula, as we have set it down, looks to a constant spiritual becoming, whereto all other things must be subordinate. The quoted utterance of Christ looks the same way. We are not to *find* our life. What is the meaning of the rather curious and unusual phrase? It means this—that to get our life out of the things which we find nearest to us and ready to our hand is to act upon a mistaken conception of life, and that life is lived rightly and wisely only when it is concerned with the making and developing of the soul within us. This is the contrast—on the one hand, the life which simply *finds* the world and all the things of the world lying round about it, and which does the best it can with these and gets the most it can out of these; and on the other hand, the life which strives and yearns and prays for a far-off greatness of soul, bends itself upon becoming something that it is not. One man settles down, so to say, among the ready-made things: here are all these material realities round about him—and he has found his life. It is all there; and all he has to do is to gather to himself as much as may be in his power to gather out of what he has found. Another man looks further and higher—feels that life is not found yet—that he is only beginning to be—that this present is to the larger future only as the bud is to the flower—that it doth not yet appear what he shall be; and he concentrates himself through all he can do of earnest effort and aspiration and prayer to produce, or to have produced, within him the life, the spiritual substance as it were, the soul enriched and greatened, which as yet are not there. And necessarily, it is among those who do not *find* their life, but who are still looking for it, that he will take his place who realises how the divine life in him is to manifest itself through, dictate to, and feed itself upon, all his relations with the world.

In all Christ's utterances upon the topic, as in this, it is the idea of a spiritual *becoming* that He takes as regulative of the disciple's dispositions toward material good. Because, for the Christian, all his relations with the material things of the world are to be at the same time a revelation and a development of the divine life within, the sense of difference between the material and the spiritual interests of life, the sense that they are in great measure opposed, must be kept ever living in the Christian's heart and mind. It was on the existence of a progressive divine life within that Christ Himself grounded His doctrine concerning the attitude of the Christian man to material things: it is on the same foundation that the Christian must ground his attitude to material things to-day.

II

On the other hand, the recognition of antagonism between spiritual and material interests must not be pushed too far—must not be pushed to the point of holding all material good as worthy of nothing but contempt and scorn. The very formula which we are taking as regulative of Christian ethics forbids; for it is a *positive* ministry which, by the formula, the developing divine life within the Christian man is to obtain from all things; and if the divine life in the Christian man were finding in all things a source of self-increase, it would necessarily preserve some sort of positive contact even with those things against which it needs to be on its guard, if only for the sake of the struggle against them and the spiritual victory in which the struggle should result. So, to put it another way, the very hostility of material things becomes a ministry of spiritual good to the Christian man only as he conquers them, not by avoiding them and dismissing them so far as possible from his life, but by keeping them in their rightful place and forcing them to their rightful use.

The Christian contention is not that material success or material comfort is wrong in itself. The curious fanaticism which every now and then rises up, holding it a sin to bestow any attention upon the material side of life, despising all material good as being unworthy of the thought of those who have heard the Christian call, is really as unchristian after its fashion as excessive attention to lower requirements is in another way. The legitimate doctrine—the doctrine which naturally emerges when we make the ethical question, as previously said, a question of spiritual biology—is simply that life's interests must be rightly ranked, and that in a true ranking of life's interests material cares drop into wholly subordinate place. It is by the struggle to keep material interests where they ought to be that the inner life strengthens itself; and the struggle, with the spiritual benefit it may bring, can only be carried on when material interests are permitted at least standing-room. That they will ceaselessly press for more, is true; but it is precisely by the Christian's discipline and restraint of them that he makes them serve the highest interests of all. It is by the wrestle with them that the soul grows.

What needs to be realised, for the purposes of a sound Christian ethical scheme, is that sacrifice has no value except as a means to a positive spiritual advance. Intrinsically, it is vanity. Every now and again the Christian Church is swept by a tide of emotion which carries it into an advocacy of sacrifice for its own sake, and into a passionate declaration that any partaking in the material good of life beyond the merest necessities of the body's sustenance is something actually approaching to a sin. The great thing, it is then contended, is to reduce life, on that side of it, to its lowest terms. Occasionally the thing is carried further still, and hardship is not only looked on as an experience to be endured with patience when God is pleased to send it, but as an experience which is to be actually sought after and is in itself a sign of grace. Satisfaction of human instinct in any form is held to be at least a weakness, if not something worse. A wave of something which one hardly likes to call sentimentalism, although it is to be feared that in many cases it is not much more, sweeps periodically over the Church, bearing it into a conviction that the sum and substance of Christian ethics consists in the giving up what has been held dear. Both the ancient and the modern worlds have seen this spirit in their midst—the spirit which supposes that the voluntary embracing of deprivation and loss, the actual going forth to seek them, must be the loftiest virtue the Christian soul can show.

The thing may easily become a delusion and a snare. In so far as the advent of this spirit is a sign of an awakened conscience, of a realisation on the part of the Church that material things have bulked too largely in its thought, it is to be welcomed; but it must be remembered that Christian ethics, as we are dealing with it, is a positive, not merely a negative thing, and is to have a very decided reaction on life. One may be self-sacrificing in act without having the haughtiness of the spirit or the pride of the heart in any wise brought down—that is, it is not necessarily the divine life within that is manifesting itself in and developing itself through an outwardly self-sacrificing act; and the Christian, even while he performs the sacrifice, may not be securing any action or reaction between the outward conduct and the inward condition. The enrichment of the heart may not follow from the impoverishment and emptying of the hand. In the passage whereof we spoke before, Christ Himself demands the losing of life, it is true—but only for His sake. There must be a positive spiritual reaction and result, else the losing is of no avail. And this is too often forgotten. It is, indeed, strange to see how those who would denounce as pernicious error any doctrine of penances, in its Roman Catholic shape, have returned to that same doctrine in varied form, and have invested with spiritual efficacy and spiritual worth an external act which may be not at all an index to the hidden soul. It is not by despising and spurning the material gain which may be put into our hands, any more than by sweeping avariciously into our hands all material gain we can, that we shall best cultivate the soul. And it is by making the cultivation of the soul, the development of the divine life within it, the paramount consideration, that the Christian man must endeavour to see his way amid the tangle of material interests through which his path winds on. It is, let it be repeated, as a question of spiritual biology that the ethical question must be faced. And treating it thus, we reach the conclusion that the *positive* spiritual ministry of material interests is secured, not when material interests are thrust aside (only a *negative* ministry is in that way obtained) but when they are yielded precisely their just place, and when all their pretension to more important place is rigidly denied.

III

What it really comes to is that the Christian man is to maintain an attitude of independence and detachment towards material circumstances, so far as the *essence* of his life is concerned. He is to touch and use them when they present themselves, yet is not to let the ever-varying countenance wherewith they look upon him affect him at the centres of his being. It is not care for them, it is not scorn for them, but indifference toward them—the indifference which does not heed how they may shape themselves, since it is not what they intrinsically are, but the spiritual purpose whereto contact with them may be turned, that constitutes the important thing—it is this indifference toward them that the Christian man is to feel. For this is the attitude toward material things which the divine life within, did it hold perfect sway, would preserve; and the Christian man, in the making of his ethical adjustments, is to set himself where and how the divine life within would set him if he were but a passive instrument in its hands. He is to live detached from trouble about external things, so that he may be free to give himself to the things that are higher. He is simply to let them be and to compel them to let him be, so that in that spirit and atmosphere of contented indifference the soul may grow. He is to be so established in the spiritual realm that he can let things come and go as they will, remaining unshaken from his rock of peace and content whatever the moment's visitation and condition may be. He is to look as if from afar upon all that takes place in the material environment girding him round. It is to appear to him as though the material life were hardly related to the essential spirit in him at all, not that he despises it, but that it almost appears to be living itself out in another world with which he has little concern. He is to let the lower processes of living go on, he being content to know nor gain nor loss, but holding himself free to concentrate upon the best.

If it be said that the counsel is hard, inasmuch as this spirit is the most difficult of all to cultivate, the answer is clear. In the Christian man, the wish to set himself as God's life within would set him if it had all its will, has a dynamic force that makes for its own fulfilment; for it does but look toward the continuation and completion of a process already begun. It has been previously stated that the *idea* of a divine life within is capable of a right regulative power only when the *fact* of it is at any rate in part a real and present thing. But if that condition be fulfilled, the idea obtains a dynamic and self-realising strength. So the desire for this spirit of contented indifference tends unfailingly to fulfil itself. Whoso wants to find the world and the world's dealings with him unimportant will surely do so. Whoso yearns to free himself from too close earthly relationships in order that he may find his true life in the interests of the soul, will by his very yearning find a curtain drawn between the world and him so that he will scarce see the earthly vision nor feel the earthly touch nor know whether it be poverty or riches the world assigns him for his lot. For as to look upon the sun makes the eye powerless to distinguish down upon the levels of earth so long as the influence of the glory persists, so does the gaze fixed upon the spiritual blot out all the rest. "Let me be detached from the lower and consecrated to the higher—indifferent to the material through being set upon that which is above—letting the outward life order itself as it may while the inward life engrosses me!" That is to be the constant desire and the constant prayer—

and the very uplifting of the prayer uplifts with it the soul into realms where the material is nothing and the spiritual is all in all.

The sum of the Christian ethical counsel, so far as concerns the Christian's relation to material things, is therefore this. Recognise the material side of living, but keep the spiritual side in the exalted place—do not, as men are so apt to do, reverse the thing, merely recognising the spiritual, while holding the material supreme. The Christian disciple, faithful in all his toiling for the bread that perisheth, receiving gladly whatever of success may result from his toil, will still turn his soul's master-passion on things that this world knows not of. For thus will it come to be ever truer for him and of him that the divine life within him manifests itself through and develops itself by all his relations with the outward and material world.

IV

(B) THE CHRISTIAN AND THE SECULAR WORLD

There is, however, a wider aspect of the general question—the aspect which regards, not so much the Christian's relation to his own material good, as his relation to the movement of the secular world as a whole. How is the Christian man to bear himself toward that mass of interests, toward all those currents of activity, toward all those ideals and purposes, which prevail beyond the Christian boundaries? Is he to hold himself in any definite relation, or in no definite relation, to these? And if in any, what is that relation to be?

We begin as we began in the consideration of the Christian and his relation to material good. As the Christian has to recognise that between the divine life within him and the material interests of his life a certain antagonism exists, so must he recognise a similar antagonism between the divine life within him and the general movement of the world. The divine life itself, were it actually, as well as ideally, the sole power constituting the Christian man, would make the recognition. In so far as it is present, it always does so. And the Christian man, treating the ethical question as one of spiritual biology, as the unfettered divine life within him would treat it, must make the recognition, too.

To be a Christian, then, in anything like the real and full significance of the word, necessitates the arming of ourselves against the spirit which is dominant in the world, and absolutely prevents us from keeping quite unruffled and smooth and sweet our relations with those who have not obeyed the Christian call. If it seem a hard saying, it has at any rate high authority to back it up: " Think not that I came to send peace on the earth. I came not to send peace, but a sword. For I came to set a man at variance against his father, and the daughter against her mother . . . and a man's foes shall be they of his own household." No picture of idyllic peacefulness did Christ himself draw as He outlined the results which allegiance to Him would bring about. He foresaw, rather, how those who owned Him for their Lord would often be driven into an attitude of uncompromising opposition toward the general sentiment and ideal of the world in which they lived. He foresaw how the life whereof He was going to be the source in man must realise itself as antagonistic to life which flows from their sources. And this was no doctrine for an earlier age, a doctrine destined to have less and less of force as the ages went on, but a doctrine abidingly true for all time. No developments of civilisation—no softening down of the superficial roughnesses of men's manners and modes of life —none of the advantages of intellect and culture and morality which are the world's boast and pride—alter, or ever will alter, the fundamental fact that life as the average sentiment of any particular time conceives it and makes it is an entirely different thing from life as Christ conceives it and as Christ makes it, and that he who declares himself as accepting the Christian ideal ought to see in the common ideals which satisfy many around him a great deal from which he must hold aloof. This lies really in the nature of things. If the Christian method is to live for goodness and for God, allowing all the lower instincts only to pick up what crumbs of satisfaction their utter subordination to goodness and to God allows them to find (and it is thus, surely, that the divine life in man would declare its aims)—and if the conventional method is to live for self so far as one dares, giving to goodness and to God just so much title to interfere as one feels one must—is not that a contrast great as any contrast can be? Christianity is, indisputably, the adoption of a spirit of life which is diametrically opposed to all the tendencies the world follows and to all the influences the world puts forth.

The true disciple, therefore, will need the soldier-spirit toward the world, since he moves amid influences and ideals which are his foes. He will, if he realises the necessities of the positon, be a man, made not wholly of pliability and complacency and power to ingratiate himself, but of sterner stuff—of watchfulness, resolution, in a sense even hardness, seriousness, alert and armed manhood. Whoso is a Christian in truth will look with something of sternness out upon the world, will keep himself in posture of defence, remembering that all these spirits he discerns moving near are spirits which would harm him did he permit their approach. Only as he understands that he moves through this world as through an alien country, wherein vigilance must never be relaxed and arms must be ever ready, only so has he realised the responsibility he undertook together with the disciple's name. That between the Christian ideal and the conventional ideal of the world there can be no compromise nor truce—that stern fact must the Christian man be prepared to face. He must be the watchful sentinel, lest he be assailed and overthrown by that world-spirit which is never far away.

In one way, perhaps, it is hardly necessary to insist so strongly upon the point since it is an accepted commonplace (whatever may be its effect or lack of effect upon Christian conduct in general) that between the Christian spirit and the world-spirit there must be at least an armed neutrality, and frequently actual war. But what is aimed at here, as in the previous instance of the Christian's relation to material good, is to show how the fact of this antagonism is fundamental and inevitable, if a system of Christian ethics be rightly grounded. We arrive, it is true, by the route we are taking, at the same idea as is reached by travellers over other routes. But we link the idea with the essential process of the

Christian life, rationalise it by so doing, and give it a stronger hold. The Christian man is to order his ways as though the divine life were manifesting itself in and developing itself through its relations with the outside world —and this means that the Christian must set himself in that attitude of opposition toward the world's ideals which the divine life, had it all initiative in its own keeping, would ceaselessly adopt.

V

This does not mean, however, that the Christian is to seclude himself from the world as far as it is possible so to do. Once again, it has to be pointed out that the Christian is to make his ethical adjustments, so far as he makes them from his own initiative, as the divine life within him would make them if his initiative were surrendered to that divine life's grasp. And the divine life, manifesting itself through, dictating to, and developing itself by, the ethical activities of every hour, would have no fear of the secular world, and, while recognising its hostility and the divergence of its ideals, would be in the world though not of it, and would certainly not run away. Since the world in some measure thrusts itself upon the field, thus making some relation with it inevitable, the fact that the inner life is to develop itself through that inevitable relationship points rather to an acceptance and mastery of it than to an effort at abolishing it so far as such a thing may be. It is thus, therefore, that the Christian man must formulate his programme in regard to the world at large.

Two opposed methods of ordering the conduct of life in this matter have always shown themselves in Christian history since Christian history began. Some seek, for their soul's sake, to avoid contact with the external world so far as such avoidance is possible: looking upon the common affairs and the common interests and the common societies of human life as forming, in the general geography of things, a sort of unhealthful district whence all manner of poisonous airs are sure to blow, they keep at as great a distance from all these things as they can, at any rate doing no more than skirt the edges of the infected land; and when necessity compels them, as it sometimes will, to make an excursion into the danger-zone, they carefully muffle themselves, before setting out, in some cloak of what others might call sanctimoniousness, which will serve, they hope, to render them safe from attack. There are people who refuse—or go as near as they can to refusing—to see or hear, or even know, what goes on in the general haunts of men. And contrasted with this is the method of those who mingle freely with the activities of the great world, who believe that on the whole, notwithstanding certain risks, it is better to let the general life press up close against the particular individual life, and whose aim is rather to maintain the soul pure amid all the temptations involved in this procedure than to secure for it the artificial and inferior safety which seclusion may bring.

That something is to be said for the method of seclusion, it is not necessary to deny. It has at any rate an appearance of spiritual thoroughness: it gives an air of sanctity to those who adopt it: it emphasises the essential separateness between religious and secular ideals. But on the other hand, the method of preserving the soul's health, not away from, but in the midst of, and if need be in spite of, all the influences of the world, produces a type of character more robust and virile than the other, and it is, besides, more in accord with the idea that a true man proves himself, not by being taken out of the world, but by being kept from the evil. And the Christian method of ethics, as we have it before us, would repeat with added force some of the objections to the system of seclusion which even ordinary observation suggests.

Treating the ethical question as a question of spiritual biology—in other words, making his ethical adjustments as the divine life within him would make them, did it have all the management of life in its own power—the Christian man must, for one thing, reckon with this outstanding fact. In programmes of life which include anything like an isolated and secluded culture of the soul, there lies an undoubted danger—the danger that the soul is being unfitted, as under a similar policy the body becomes unfitted, for the sudden changes of temperature and atmosphere which at some time or other are bound to come. The idea of secluding the inner life from all, or nearly all, the influences radiating out of the general life of men cannot, after all, be carried out: suddenly the moment is sure to announce itself when, for some reason not to be denied or evaded, the man who has hitherto contrived to keep his life free from many points of contact with the larger life outside is compelled to go forth on the ways where the crowds are gathered; and he will there feel all the greater strangeness, be all the more unable to adjust himself to the new conditions, for his unaccustomedness to the road. The conditions of life make it impossible that any man should permanently stand apart. Every individual is too deeply involved in the great whole. The recluse, long as he may succeed in escaping the temptations which find their hunting-ground out in the populated centres of life, has to quit his retirement at length; and his soul, having developed no powers of resistance, being unpractised in the cut and thrust of spiritual warfare, is the more likely to succumb. The method of cherishing the soul's health in some carefully guarded and hermetically sealed chamber produces in the soul a debility which exposes it to double danger when it faces, as face it must, the stronger blasts it has not previously been permitted to feel. From the point of view of the development of life, therefore—the point of view which the Christian man must endeavour to take—the method of seclusion fails to secure the safety which at a superficial glance it may seem likely to win, and becomes a method of actual danger and loss. Which is to say that in the light of the idea of a developing divine life it stands out as a method to be condemned rather than praised.

It has to be added, besides, that the life of God in man would never consent to look upon the great world as if God Himself had withdrawn from it, and would hold such a procedure as a betrayal of its own claims. The Christian man must consequently admit that the method of seclusion, the method of marking off the larger part of human life as out of bounds, is really faithless, implying that God has practically withdrawn from the general order of things and left evil in undisputed possession of the field. It is indeed pessimism of the most extreme kind to hold that out in the wide realms where men are fulfilling their purposes and ideals, out among the different impulses whereby the masses of men are moved, out in the region of jostling personalities and gathered thoughts and crowded wills and closely-packed activities—that out there nothing is to be met with but what is evil! Such despair of the general system of things could hardly consist, surely, with a religion founded on faith in a living God! The method of self-seclusion from the general movement of the world is essentially and practically atheistic, indignantly as it would repudiate the charge; for it assumes that God has abandoned His own creation, has died to all interest in and all control over the multiplex businesses of the creatures whom He has made. And this, which is the conclusion at which ordinary reasoning about the matter would arrive, becomes emphasised as the only right conclusion when we survey the matter from the standpoint of the divine life and the verdicts it would pronounce. The divine life would not abandon the world to the sway of wrong, nor take up any attitude toward the world which implied that such an abandonment had been made. It would rather claim all the world for its own. And the Christian man must make a similar claim for himself and for the divine life by which in part he is made.

It is admitted, of course, that for the Christian

man, at his present level of experience, there lies, in contact with the world and in mingling with its activities, a risk which would not be incurred were he wholly surrendered to an initiative higher than his own. And clearly, therefore, it is not the part of wisdom to go forth into the great world without taking precautions for spiritual safety. But just as it was stated, in the treatment of the previous question, that the desire for the spirit of contented indifference toward material good tends to bring about its own fulfilment, so in the present connection a statement on similar lines may be made. The desire to live, in regard to the world at large, as the unfettered divine life within would dictate, tends also to fulfil itself, and, while driving the Christian man into all legitimate contacts with the world, will keep him back from all contacts that could harm. To put it in another way, if the Christian man, failing the perfect regulative effect of the *fact* of the life of God, allows the *idea* of it to have regulative power, he will be in large degree prepared to face the risks which his contact with the world is bound to involve. To be constantly possessed by that idea in sincerity is to put the nature through a process—rather, to keep it constantly undergoing a process—whereby it is fitted to endure the various influences impinging upon it from the secular world. The Christian man, in so far as he retains the ethical government of his world-relations within his power, will keep that government on right lines by earnestly and persistently willing to order it as it would be ordered if the divine life were all in all. The will to do so is itself a safeguard—both an inspiration and a restraint. A certain risk remains, it is true. But one need not be afraid to say that the soul which would be great must take some risks. And we come back, at the end of the matter, to a point closely kindred with one insisted on in the previous chapter—that the finest Christian achievement is to show the distinctive Christian quality upon the common ways. So may we say now that it is a nobler achievement to make and keep something approaching to sainthood among so many things which in their malevolence seem bent upon tripping and spoiling it, than to make and keep it in a seclusion where bolts and bars hold temptations at bay. This, at any rate, is the Christian's call.

VI

One other point remains in connection with the Christian's relation to the world at large. If he seek to adjust that relation as though the divine life were manifesting itself in it, dictating to it, and developing itself from it, he will be driven, not only into the *defensive* hostility towards the world of which we have previously spoken, but into an *aggressive* hostility which endeavours to win and overcome the world's evil and bring the world into captivity to the good. This, assuredly, is what the divine life would do; and the Christian must adopt for himself and on his own account, must identify himself with, the movement which the divine life would make. The ordinary doctrine that it is a Christian's duty to set himself into open warfare with the evil that is in the world (once again, a commonplace of Christian ethics, like the other doctrines spoken of in this chapter) becomes doubly strong in its appeal, and infinitely more binding, when set in the light of that regulative principle whereby, as we are throughout insisting, Christian activity is to be directed and inspired.

The Christian spirit, therefore, is aggressive in regard to all the unchristian spirits whereof the world is full; and it will not be content unless the one right method of living which it believes itself to have found is being pressed upon the acceptance of those that follow other methods; and whoso calls himself by the Christian name must realise that he has not only to guard himself against the evil infection of the world, but has to see to it that his own better influence shall infect the world. The Christian has not only a defence to maintain: he has an aggressive and offensive warfare to wage. And the quieter and more gracious aspects of the Christian system of life, important as they are, must not be so exclusively emphasised that this truth becomes obscured. It is worth noting that in the life which is governed and ordered according to the Christian method, there is room for well-nigh every instinct which finds a place in human nature—room, at any rate, for every instinct transfigured and transformed, purged of its base alloy and refined to purer gold. The instincts and impulses wherewith man works out his tragedies and his crimes are seized upon by the Christian spirit, when man submits, and lo! those impulses and instincts become the very instruments wherewith man may hasten the coming of the kingdom of God. That old fighting instinct, that sheer love of battle, that rejoicing in a death-grapple with an implacable foe—which is one of the instincts whereby, in its untransformed and primitive condition, man is brought nearest to the brutes—becomes, in its Christianised shape, one of the things whereby man is set closest to God. In the life rightly adjusted according to the Christian ethical method, there is room even for that—more even than room, rather an actual demand and call. The Christian must do battle on behalf of the sovereignty of good against all usurpers filling the thrones that good should occupy; and in his heart there must be—if he realises what is involved in the spiritual condition he claims to have reached—a passionate impatience with all that the divine life forbids or disapproves, an eagerness to smite down whatsoever is an offence in its eyes. The Christian is to be, not only the frontier-guard who permits no enemy to pass, but the knight of a holy chivalry who goes forth to challenge all that does not yield to the supreme and rightful claim.

There is a bigotry of which the Christian world has shown far too much—the bigotry of mere opinion, intolerant of intellectual conclusions different from its own. There is a proud aggressiveness of which the Christian world has shown far too little—the proud aggressiveness of those who realise that the spirit they seek to obey is the one spirit with a right to the obedience of all. The Christian conduct of life, one needs to reiterate and insist, is not completely attained unless something of that aggressiveness enter in. The Christian who has never, in all charity and yet in all firmness, sought to make evil ashamed of itself—who has never, with entire absence of pride in himself, and yet with fulness of pride in the cause to which, as partaker of the divine life of God through Christ, he is vowed, declared by deed or word, in the sight or hearing of others, that wrong shall not have its way—who has never, through firmness of attitude or resoluteness of speech, struck one good blow upon the foul spirits that are ever rearing their heads—is not worthy to bear the Christian name. The Christian must be conscious of, and must fight for, that royalty and that majesty which inhere in the very life of God—the life which has already in part supplanted his own, and to the lines of whose activity he seeks to conform whatever activities of his own may still remain. Only so does the divine life in him both manifest itself through and develop itself from his contacts with the hostile ideals of the world.

VII

(C) THE CHRISTIAN AND THE SHORTNESS OF LIFE

Nothing has hitherto been said concerning the brevity of this present life as a fact to be taken into account by the Christian in adjusting his attitude toward the things of the world. That the fact has significance in this connection is generally admitted and understood; and inasmuch as this life is even as a vapour that passes away, the Christian is exhorted not to bind himself too closely and fervently to its interests, but to fix his heart upon the things that are above. The things that are seen are temporal, and the things that are not seen are eternal. And for this reason, the

Christian is to sit loosely to all earthly affairs, to withdraw his gaze from that which is immediate and near and to fix it upon the far horizons where time melts into eternity, remembering always that his citizenship is in heaven.

That the shortness of life is indeed to be a regulative factor in the Christian's self-adjustment to the world is, from our present point of view, as from any other that can claim to be rational, to be admitted as an indisputable truth. What we have now to do is to relate the truth to the general line of thought which in these pages we are following out, to show its basis, and perhaps to make some qualification in the deduction ordinarily drawn—the deduction that with a realisation of life's transiency interest in this present life must of necessity fade.

Clearly (and this is the first thing to be grasped) he whose supreme interest lies in the development of the eternal life within him must have a vivid and abiding consciousness of how fleeting are all the things of time. It is, so to say, part of the essential self-realisation of the divine life in man that it should ceaselessly apprehend the transiency of the material stage on which for the time being it performs its part. It must necessarily know itself as enduring: it must necessarily know the world as passing away; and the two contrasting and yet complementary facts must be ever present to its apprehension. A life which at the same time manifests itself in and develops itself through—acts upon and is reacted upon by—its relations with the world must keep firm grip upon the cardinal realities of the situation, since only as they are rightly and vividly apprehended do those realities react upon life in a way that makes for good. The Christian, therefore, making the idea of a developing life within him regulative of his ethical attitudes, must similarly remind himself—must not shirk the fact or attempt to thrust it below the line of sight—that the fashion of the world passeth away.

It is probably true to say that the idea of life's brevity is an idea which we try to keep off as far as we can. Life is short, certainly—but why notice the fact before we are obliged to do so? There is too much sadness in it: it is one of those things about which, for the sake of our own happiness, the less said the better. It will force itself upon us soon enough—till then, let it be forgotten, or, if that cannot be, let us at any rate pretend that it is forgotten. Though the enemy approaches, let us at least refuse to speak his name. If he be looking upon us from his ambush, waiting for his moment to spring upon us and make us his prey, we will not look that way. This is the attitude of most. And it is the attitude of the generality of religious men and women, no less than of others: their profession of faith in Christianity and in Christ, although they may say that it robs death of its sting, does not make them any the more willing to grow familiar with the company of the idea; and the Christian keeps at a distance the thought —the sad, dread thought, as even he considers it—of the quick and sure slipping past of the days.[1]

Obviously, it is quite impossible to make the best use, for purposes of spiritual development, of the position in which we stand, so long as we thus leave one of its essential elements out of the reckoning. If there be a term set for us a little way ahead, the fact ought somehow to influence our mood and conduct, our entire moral posture, at every moment till the term is reached; and we lose the influence it ought to have, if we thrust the thought of it aside. If the days be numbered for us, life ought surely to be a different thing —differently ordered, differently inspired, with different ideals and with all its emphasis falling on different places—than it would be if the days had no appointed bound; and he who gets as near as he can to living as though the days *had* no

---

[1] Rudyard Kipling makes one of his characters say, not very elegantly, but with only too much of truth, "How these Christians funk death!"

appointed bound, will find his life, to say the least of it, deformed, and the emphasis of his living wrongly set. The inner life cannot work itself out on right lines or to true issues (and it is from the point of view of life's development, from the point of view of spiritual biology, that this question, like all the rest, is to be considered) if one of the most commanding facts of the situation be expelled from its place in our thought. A life from above, permeating and penetrating the lower life of man, would most assuredly find in the transiency of the present system of things one of the cardinal points of its compass, so to say—one of the outstanding truths by which its self-adjustment would be set. The Christian man, governing himself by the idea of the development of life within, must similarly make himself familiar with the fact of the brevity of his connection with earthly things; for only as its brevity is recognised can that connection become a factor making for an inner development that is true. Life's shortness is not a fate which he is to forget so long as he can: it is a fact to be faced and used— a fact neither good nor bad except as his use of it makes it one or the other—a fact from which it is his business to draw some influence and effect back upon every passing day. Only so does he set himself in the same relation to the fact as that in which he would be set by a divine life manifesting itself in and feeding itself upon its relations with the world.

VIII

It is necessary, however, that the shortness of life should be remembered in the right spirit, and that, when remembered, it should produce the right result. For remembrance of the fact may operate in mistaken ways; and the Christian man must see to it that he faces the fact as the divine life itself would face it—as it would be faced by a life both manifesting itself in and developing itself through its attitude to the transitory world. And this at once excludes the method of those who say (with what sincerity or absence of sincerity need not here be discussed) that, because life is short, life is worthless too; who declare that they are longing with eager passion for the day when earthly things shall trouble them no more; who do their best to make all hearers understand that, whatever any one else may be, they at least are only pilgrims and strangers here; who revel in a sort of sentimental sorrow that they were ever unfortunate enough to stray into this world at all. The underlying idea in all this is that the true soul *puts up with* life because it must, but is glad to hurry through it with all possible speed. The inference is that because this life is a thing soon to pass, and a thing which does not seem to come to very much, it is therefore a thing to be lightly esteemed, if not despised.

It is not thus that a divine life, manifesting itself in and feeding itself upon all its world-relations, would take the case. It is not in this attitude, therefore, that the Christian man must set himself. The formula points first, it is true, to a refusal to identify life with the things of earth and time, since they come but to pass away; but it points, next, to an actual renewal of interest, from the spiritual point of view, in the things of earth and time, and to a determination that, although they themselves do not abide, they shall be made to work some moral education in us which shall abide when they themselves are gone. Whoso rightly learns the lesson of life's change and life's decay and life's swiftly approaching close, will first lose interest in all the contents of life for what they are in themselves, but will then come back to them and clasp them and sound them and hold fast to them, with fresh interest in the opportunity of spiritual training and growth—an opportunity so short and so soon to be gone—which they afford. Life is short—not worth troubling about very much, then. That may well be the first word. But life is short— then all the more eagerly must its experiences be cared for, and all the more fully must they be lived through, and all the greater must interest

CHRISTIAN'S RELATION TO WORLD

in them grow, lest there be hidden in them some offer of spiritual education which we do not accept—an offer which the quickly moving years bear further and further from us, and which can never return. That must be the next word. The inference is not that, because life is brief, life is worthless too. The inference is that, because life is brief, it has all the greater worth. Every second ticks off something from the duration of the spiritual opportunity which lies before us; and we must waken all the keener interest in life's duties and responsibilities and relationships, that we may make the most, for our spiritual culture, of the time we have. They who treat the matter of life's swift passing from the point of view of spiritual biology, will be hungering and athirst to taste life to the full—not that in itself it is a thing to which they would be bound, but that out of all its experience, rightly embraced and worthily used, the soul may learn and grow. For the inner life is to *feed itself upon and develop itself from* its relations with the transitory world. The sense of how swiftly life passes is not to kill life's interest or to make life a worthless thing in our eyes, but to impart to it an interest higher, purer, and therefore keener too, than it ever possessed before. For every detail and every engagement of it may have some moral and spiritual reaction upon the character we bear; and the very swiftness of its passing should cause us to see to it all the more earnestly that none of its spiritual possibilities be missed.

Mere detachment from life on the ground of its transiency is not the attitude which Christian ethics prescribes. Detachment from life for what it is in itself may come first; but there must follow a using and a probing of life for whatever it may have to give toward the perfecting of the soul. Detachment—yet use: it is to a union of the two that the true consideration of the matter should lead. Many try to detach themselves from life in a manner and in a measure, realising that because it does not endure, it cannot be a thing to which the heart should cling; but they fail to understand that it is a thing filled through and through with spiritual uses, and that therefore —precisely because it does not endure—it must be all the more earnestly lived while it is here. Consecration to highest ideals sets us free from the things of this our present life—true. But consecration to highest ideals brings us back into contact—though it be a different and finer contact—with the things of this our present life once more. For they are the instruments whereby the highest ideals are to be wrought out—the steps on which we climb heavenward—the earthly food which the spirit in us is to transmute into health and strength of soul.

CHRISTIAN'S RELATION TO WORLD 171

So must the Christian man use the fact of the shortness of life for his good. So is he in the world and yet not of it, one of its keenest citizens and yet with his home in heaven. So does he conquer death—not fearing it and yet not desiring by one instant to hasten its steps, indifferent when it may befall, so that it does but find life's spiritual opportunity used to the full. So does he adjust his own attitude as the divine life within him would adjust it if it had all its power. And so does he, in at least one of the important affairs of Christian ethics, bring the ideal governing it into closest relation with the one supreme ideal that ought to govern all.

VII

THE CHRISTIAN'S RELATION TO HIS FELLOW-MEN

WE pass from the topic of the Christian's relations with the world to that of his relations with his fellow-men. And we treat it by the same method, as a question of spiritual biology, asking how the matter would be dealt with by a divine life manifesting itself through the ethical situations of every day, and remembering that the Christian, so far as he retains the ethical initiative of his life in his own hands, is to order things as the divine life within him would order them if it had perfect sway. It is to be noted, however, that in dealing with this subject we have the advantage of being able to make a much more immediate and direct use of the example of Jesus Christ than is possible in many other cases; and this fact will assist and govern us in our dealing with the theme. In the great majority of ethical questions it is scarcely possible to find in the life of Christ a situation which, in its setting, in its outward conditions, corresponds with exactness to our own: the whole method and object of His life removed Him far from many of the matters which bulk most largely in the lives of ordinary men; and while one may be able to run lines of connection from the *spirit* which He manifested in His own sphere to the *spirit* which we ought to manifest in ours, and thus obtain some guidance, anything like an actual *imitation* is out of the question, because no actual example has been set. And there is, besides, the fact that the developing history of the world has given rise to many ethical problems which had no existence at all in the time of Christ. The system of Christian ethics which adopts the formula "Imitate Christ" as all-sufficing is bound to find that on many of the most pressing modern themes its formula yields no help. But here, as regards the relations of the Christian to his fellow-men, as regards the law of Love and the principles whereby its application should be regulated, the matter is altogether different. Here Christ occupied the same position as we occupy. The factors of the situation are identical for Him and for us. Not the uniqueness of Christ's Person, not the altogether special character of His ministry, not the changes in the constitution of society which the intervening centuries have wrought, put any distance between Him and us in this regard. He worked, so far as this matter is concerned, on the same stage, and had the same part to sustain. He wrought in the same material, used the same colours, had the same canvas before Him. And we can therefore refer back for an example to the story of his life, confident that that example will be waiting for us there, only needing to be drawn out into the light and surveyed with attentive and obedient regard. In this sphere of the mutual relations of men we can make our lives a reproduction of the life of Jesus as it is in no other sphere possible for us to do; for in this sphere, as in hardly any other, He lived precisely *our* life. Side by side, then, with the statement that the Christian man is to adjust his relations with his fellows as the divine life within him would adjust them if it had perfect sway, we set the other statement that he is to adjust them as Christ adjusted His. Or rather, we may say that in the life of Christ we have a perfect concrete instance of the working out of the formula which the first statement contains. For His Father worked "hitherto," and He worked; and it was by the divine life in Him that all the doing of Christ was really done.

I

(*A*) THE LAW OF LOVE

It is not necessary to prove that the first law of men's mutual relations, according to the Christian ethical system, is the law of love. This is accepted as an axiom by every one who claims to understand Christianity or to bear the Christian name. What is necessary, however, is to see how from our present standpoint the law is grounded, and how much more binding and far-reaching it becomes. The Christian is to be set toward men as the divine life is set toward them: his spirit toward them is to be that of God in him; and it is on the fact that God is Love, and that the Christian's ethical attitudes and movements are to reproduce the attitudes and movements of God, that the obligation to brotherly kindness is based. We are taken, that is to say, on this view, beyond mere generalities about human brotherhood—generalities which are inspiring enough in the sound of them, but which not seldom break down and lose their power precisely when the critical moment of testing arrives. It is not so much the fact that he is the brother of his fellow-men, and is therefore bound to show him honour, render him service, and keep for him a warm place in his heart—true as these things are—from which the Christian starts. This fact becomes rather the fact at which he arrives—having started from the other fact that the life of God, which is a life of love, is in part the life that makes him, and that his ethical activities are, so far as he himself guides them, to be adjusted as the life of God, which is a life of love, would adjust them if it made him wholly. Brotherhood, in other words, is the love of God at one remove; and it is obligatory upon the Christian man, not so much *per se,* as being involved in the fact that God, with His lovingness, dwells within him, and that the idea of this in-dwelling is to be regulative of all the Christian's ways. The Christian man will be loving brother to men, not so much because he looks to men as because he looks to God. God is in him in part: for the rest, he must bear himself as though God were in him wholly; and God is Love.

It was thus, in fact, that Christ grounded His own attitude of tenderness and service toward men. His relations with men were what they were because of His relations with God: love, in Him, was simply His oneness with the Father working itself out in its natural consequences on the side of His human connections; and one need not fear to say that His graciousness toward men was due, not so much to the claims of mankind without Him, as to the claims of God within Him. The ordinary phrases concerning brotherhood seldom or never came from His lips. It was not from that centre that He worked. Somewhat remarkable this may appear to be, when we remember how Christ was the perfect example of kindness in love and ministry to suffering and needy men, and how He is universally so acclaimed to-day; but the fact is so. One cannot read the Gospels

without feeling that what Christ did for men—
all His offices of help and healing, all His charities, all His "mighty works" on men's behalf—
came directly out of His perfect surrender to the
divine life, were motived in that, flowed out of
that as a stream flows from its source. Man's
need drew mercy from Him, true; but it did so
primarily because He was one with the Father.
It was, indeed, to that oneness that man's need
made its appeal. Christ's union with God implied
love. Christ's love was that union acting itself
out in a particular way and within a particular
sphere. This it is that gives a touch of something like austerity (though the word is scarcely
a happy one, and is employed only in default of
a better) even to the most helpful and engaging
ministries Christ wrought. The frenzied enthusiasm of brotherhood, so frequently commended
to-day as being the supreme manifestation of the
Christian spirit, is never there. It is always
toward God—toward the Source of the life in
Him—that Christ is looking, even when it is
upon man that His healing hands are laid. Confronted by the man born blind, for example, His
word is that "We must work the works of him
that sent me, while it is day." [1] It is the pressure of the divine life within that makes, forces
out, motives, the marvellous love. Or, again, at
one of the classic passages wherein the Apostle

[1] John ix. 4.

Paul speaks of the wonderful self-abnegation of Christ for man's sake, the same thing comes out. "He humbled himself, becoming obedient even unto death"[1]—*obedient* unto death. It is of unselfishness among Christ's disciples that the apostle is writing: surely, as he points to the example Christ Himself has set, he will speak of Him as having been loving and unselfish even unto death! But no—*obedient* is the word. The moving impulse in Christ's self-sacrifice was primarily in His relation of utter obedience to every inspiration His Father sent Him; which is but another way of saying that it was in His relation of entire oneness with His Father's life. His very love to man was itself a consequence of—rather, another aspect of—His intimate union with God.

In saying that the Christian is to make the idea of the divine life within him regulative of his attitude toward his fellows we are, therefore, bidding the Christian do what Christ Himself did—save, of course, that with Christ it was never the mere *idea,* but always the *fact,* that performed the controlling work. And the lesson for the Christian on this matter is twofold. First, let the divine life, so far as it is within you, and the idea of it, so far as you still retain the ethical initiative of your life in your own keeping, order your relations with your brethren; and so you

[1] Philippians ii. 5.

will be driven into love from within, rather than drawn into it from without. And next, come back from the enthusiastic talk about brotherhood (which has its rightful place, certainly, but only as the implication in and the consequence of a larger idea, and not as being itself the idea from which the start is made) to see how much more surely the law of love is grounded when it is taken as following from the conception of a divine life energising within. Indeed, one of the lessons the world most greatly needs to learn is that we shall not keep our relations true with man unless the stress of the whole thing falls, not upon those relations, but upon our relation with the life of God. The obvious truth is that they who are really one with God will not and cannot be hardhearted toward men. The modern world thinks itself to have found, in the magic word and the magic idea of brotherhood, the force which will redeem human relationships from their sordidness, and bring peace and good-will to the tumultuous and strife-torn earth. Religion, it has discovered, has been a selfish thing: the soul has concentrated itself upon its relations with its God, forgetting its relations with its kindred souls; and the world needs that we should lay less stress upon the saving of ourselves, and exalt into greater prominence the saving of those who walk life's pathway at our side. Brotherhood, philanthropy—they are the vaunted gospel-words of the age. Perhaps one might say, by way of at any rate partial reply, that the idea of brotherhood, loudly as it may be advocated in meeting and in press, shows small power to restrain men from coming to death-grips with one another when envious or angry passions are roused; and the long-continued proclamation of it has after all done comparatively little, either in private, national or international, spheres, to make wars to cease and love supreme. It has to be confessed, on the other hand, that intensity of religious life has often gone hand in hand with hardness and self-seeking. But that could only be where the fact or idea of a divine life was not fully understood or submitted to. Wholly surrendered to the God who Himself is love, how can man be other than loving, or harden himself against those whom he is able to help? Let it be recalled once more that in Him whose spirit we are to possess and whose method we are to copy, it was the mind of obedience to God, the fact of oneness with God, that drove Him to serve and suffer for man: it was because God was all in all for Him and in Him that He became and still remains so much to us. The Christian man, making it his first concern to adjust his relations with his fellows as the divine life, if it swayed him wholly, would adjust them—making the fact or the idea of the divine life regulative in this matter as in others —will be moved, as a natural consequence, to love. It is true that human lives are bound together, and should be so thought of. It is true that every man is his brother's keeper. But it is also true that the Christian man will best keep his brethren, so far as the duty of keeping them is his, by letting the divine life keep him. The treatment of the question of human relations as a question of spiritual biology leads to the conclusion that the Christian must be—not through supplementary or inferential considerations, however powerful, but simply because he is a Christian—a man whose life toward his fellows is love. To say the second thing is, indeed, but to say the first in other words. For God is in the Christian; and God is love.

II

It will easily be seen that if the Christian's relations with his fellows are taken as thus regulated—if the law of love be taken as binding simply because it is implied in the fact of a divine life within—love becomes a much more energising, a much more constant, thing in life than it becomes under any other method of advocating its claims. For one thing, if the Christian aims at adjusting his attitude toward his brethren in the indicated way, every opportunity of service becomes a duty, a direct and binding call. For, in so far as such language can be employed of God at all, it might be said that it is thus God Himself views the matter, and it is thus, therefore, that God's life in the Christian would view them. It is not too much to declare, concerning God's relations with humanity, that God *exists for* men and the good of men: His activities of beneficence toward men are never a mere incident among other activities toward them; and wherever human need touches upon His infinite resource, wherever His infinite resource comes into contact with human need, there, as a natural consequence, love flows out from the resource upon the need. It is for purposes of love that God puts Himself in contact with human life. The Christian man, reckoning the matter in similar fashion, must take every opportunity, every possibility, of service to his fellows, as naturally implying the outflow of love. He must realise himself, whenever he is brought close, in possibility of helping or saving, to any kindred life, to be a part of that eternal movement of love which does not pick and choose, but gives itself naturally at the instant of necessity's touch. An opportunity is always more than an opportunity. It is a direct and binding call. It becomes, in this view, a part of the eternal foreordaining by which Eternal Love works out the good of the world.

RELATION TO FELLOW-MEN

It was thus that Christ Himself read the matter. "We *must* work the works of him that sent us, while it is day," He said on the occasion of that miracle to which we have previously referred. Standing there with those darkened eyes before Him, His thought takes a far-reaching range. Not "We *may*," but "We *must*." The meeting with this man was a direct call and command from the Father. There was present in Christ, not a mere sentiment of compassion, however sincere and deep—not only a passing wave of pity, however strong—not simply a loving desire to bring that maimed life relief—not only these things, though of course all these things were there—but the mighty, irresistible constraint of the knowledge that the dealing with this man was fore-ordained in the eternal Father's thought, and was part of the divinely appointed mission of the Son. And thus, always, He moved among men with no doubt as to the right place and time in which to manifest His power, with no hesitancy as to the proper channels through which His healing grace should run. Every broken life that presented itself before Him was in His eyes a command from God that there and then His power of restoration should awaken; and every soul, stricken with spiritual poverty or foul with the loathsomeness of sin—every such soul on which His tender gaze fell bore upon it, in its very poverty and sin, the proof that it had been divinely selected for the manifestation of a holy work of love.

Opportunity makes duty—the Christian who seeks to adjust himself in all things as the divine life would adjust itself and him, will take that as an established principle. And, if he takes it so, the idea of responsibility will have a very much stronger hold upon him than it has upon many. All admit, of course, that they are responsible for the exercise of holy charities toward their fellow-men: they find no difficulty in yielding assent to that general statement; but that general, diluted responsibility presses very lightly upon the majority, and moves them to few out-pourings of beneficence or help. But the thought that every instance of human need we meet and every cry we hear wrung from human lips and every tear we see falling from human eyes—that these things are *in themselves* a present witness to our present responsibility, is a much more constraining thing. And that thought follows naturally from the principle that the Christian man is to order his relations with his fellow-men as the divine life in him would order those relations if it had perfect control and power. God goes out in love naturally, by the instinctive movement of His nature (of course one speaks after the manner of men) whenever human need touches His

RELATION TO FELLOW-MEN 185

infinite resource. Translated into a Christian ethical programme, this means that for the Christian man every opportunity is a duty, a direct and binding call.

So far of actual service to our brethren. In many other ways, however, the adjustment of man's attitude to man under the regulative fact or idea of the divine life within will make human relations a sweeter and more sensitive thing, tuning them to finer harmonies than the regulative idea of brotherhood would ever bring about. For instance (and this is but one of the many lines on which the matter may be followed out), the adjustment of our attitude towards our fellow-men on the indicated principle will not seldom mean *self-repression, self-restraint*—perhaps a finer and more difficult virtue than self-sacrifice itself. The love in the life of God manifests itself as much in restraint of power as in exercise of power; and, in the classic Pauline passage alluded to earlier, we are reminded how the mind that was in Christ Jesus " counted it not a thing to be grasped to be on an equality with God," and are instructed, also, to have this mind in ourselves. It is not necessary, in order to appreciate the significance of this latter utterance, to enter into any of the more subtle theological implications which it may contain. Without that, the main point is clear. With the possibility open to Him of manifesting, in His relations to the world and to men, the very greatness and power of God Himself, the Christ kept the greatness to a large extent hidden and the power unused. He counted it not a thing to be grasped at that the strength in Him should do all it could. It is indeed, when one thinks of it, the surpassing miracle of Christ's life—not that the wonders He did were so many, but that being what He was He left so many undone, that, with power so irresistible leaping and palpitating in Him, He held it so rigidly restrained. In that sense, Christ let some of His opportunities go by. He hid within Himself the glory which, had He permitted it to shine forth, would have compelled the world to worship and adore. The restraint of power, no less than the exercise of power, is, both with God and with the Christ whom He sent, one of the highest manifestations of love.

So with the Christian, ordering himself on right principles, will it sometimes be. It is of course a far descent from the self-repression of God and Christ to any self-repression within the range of man; and yet the former is a thing which the divine life within the Christian man, or the regulative idea of the divine life, will in measure reproduce. The Christian man will take it as one of the governing ethical axioms of his life that—quite apart from any question of direct

RELATION TO FELLOW-MEN 187

service or direct harm to his fellows—the fulness of power in him is sometimes, for his brethren's sake, not to be employed. It will not be enough for him that having done all he can and obtained all he can, he should hand over to others something of what has resulted from his doing and his getting, dignifying that adjustment of the situation by the title of self-sacrifice. He will, before he begins his doing and his obtaining, remember that others enter into the calculation, and, if his relations with these require it, will leave his strength unused. Self-sacrifice, in the sense of giving up things, is not a virtue for every day, because not every day are we in possession of anything that can be given up; but self-suppression, self-restraint, the holding back of something we might do—the opportunity for that returns with far more frequent step. Even in the smallest of life's spheres it comes. In our very speech with one another the opportunity of self-repression may arise. With a word, we might perhaps assert our own wisdom and hush all reply; yet he who desires to live by the inspiration of the divine life will now and then keep silence, holding it not a thing to be grasped at to establish the superiority of his own mind. And nothing has been given: he to whom forbearance has been shown knows nothing about it and we ourselves are in no wise the poorer for the showing; yet a real Christian virtue has been brought into play. And passing from this instance, on the lowest plane as it is, to larger things, to the enterprise and activity of life, how often there come to us occasions when, with no wrong-doing, without any actual meanness for which the judgment of others could reproach us, we might win some possession we should so much like to have, reach some success which would thrill us with the glow of delight. Yet the possession and the success, did we seize them, would in some indefinable way —we could not reason it out perhaps, but the deepest voices in us declare it—rub a little of the gold of life away for others: they would not recognise it as a loss, did we exert our power and take the prize: they will not recognise it as a gain, if we obey the better impulse and hold our hand: sacrifice there will not be in the sense of giving up something which another receives; but by our grip upon ourselves we shall have kept our relationship sweet with our fellow-men. In the common intercourse of every day does the spirit of self-repression find ample opportunity. Self-sacrifice implies the possession of something valuable and rich, more or less, on the part of him who is to make the sacrifice: the spirit of self-restraint implies nothing more than that touching of one ordinary life upon other ordinary lives which is the common lot of all. And inasmuch as the restraint of power is one of the constant ways of self-manifestation that the love in the divine life adopts, the restraint of power will be one of the constant ways of self-manifestation that love adopts in the case of the Christian man. Difficult to common human nature as it may be, it will come to be the natural thing for him who adjusts himself to his fellows in such wise as he would be adjusted to his fellows by God within. For it is for this restraint of power, amid many other fine and high and seemingly subtle orderings of man's attitude to man, that the divine life will call. And we are justified in declaring, after what has been said (though the point might be emphasised in many other ways), that if the question of man's relations to man be treated as a question of spiritual biology—if the fact of the divine life within, or the idea of the divine life within, be made regulative of those relations—love becomes a much more energising, a much more constant, a much more searching and sensitive thing, than it becomes under any other method of advocating its claims.

III

It is worth noting, although it is not necessary to elaborate the point at great length, that the Christian's love for man, if it flow from the regulative action of the divine life within him in its fact or its idea, will keep the spiritual element predominant, and will thus escape a danger into which love otherwise kindled may easily fall. It will not lay all the stress upon the mere ministering to a brother's secular benefit; and reform of material conditions, though obtaining all its rights, will not be held as the only important thing, nor viewed out of its relations with the higher good. Not that the Christian man will be heedless concerning it: in this sphere, as in others, duty will arise whenever opportunity presents itself; and the Christian will be eager that the hungry shall be fed, the naked clothed, the prisons of disability opened for them that are bound, and throughout the social realm the acceptable year of the Lord ushered in. But love of the right order will remember that a view of life which takes *only* these things into account, or which dismisses other things with a mere formal recognition, is a view of life out of which the sense of true proportion has disappeared. It will remember that even reforms which are intrinsically necessary, even progress which is undoubtedly in the right direction, must not be looked on detached from the larger question of moral and spiritual condition. It will remember that man does not live by bread alone. For this is the estimate of things, as to their relative value, which the love in the divine life adopts, and is therefore the estimate which must be adopted by the love dwelling in the Christian's heart.

It is a real danger that is thus provided against. For, while welcoming every sign that Christian men are awaking to the pressing claims of social reform, rousing themselves to take up the duties which they have neglected too long, one cannot but feel that now and again the new-born love of to-day has too little of spiritual quality in it, and loses much of its value thereby. The enthusiasm of brotherhood forgets too often that the value of any reform depends, not alone upon what it is intrinsically, but upon its right relation to other things—that life is, or ought to be, a careful balance between many concerns—that a great deal of reform may come from a mistaken spirit in those who give it and address itself to a mistaken spirit in those who receive it. Strange as it may sound, love itself may be materialistic: it may be simply materialism going out upon others instead of materialism staying at home. Not seldom the idea of progress is interpreted, even by Christian men, as if it had no spiritual content. Love, even in Christian men, not seldom turns its gaze away from spiritual horizons, and sees only what is of the earth, earthy. And, while no word is to be said by way of belittling or depreciating the passion for humanity, which through these later years is at last coming to its own, the wish may at least be uttered that it possessed a more constant and fuller understanding of the ideal for whose sake it should strive. It should come to *all* its own.

From the indicated danger the Christian who adjusts his relations with men under the governance of the divine life will be kept safe. He will love, but with a love full-orbed. Love in him will be mindful that any seeming benefit which takes his brethren still further in the direction of materialistic absorption may really be a snare rather than a help. It will be mindful, through all its yearning passion, that a man's life consisteth not in the abundance of the things he possesseth— that progress divorced from vivid spiritual ideals is not worth the name—that the dominance of the spiritual, and this alone, can give ultimate and permanent value to the fair Utopias of the reformer's dreams. It will know that, without the predominance of the spiritual element, every door of material gain through which man presses, imagining himself to be getting nearer to the central chamber of perfect joy, really marks a step further to the dungeon and to doom. Through all its ministry it will hold man's spiritual interests to be supreme. The bread that perisheth it will give when it can; but the bread of life will be a yet more important thing in its regard. In the long run, nothing will matter to it—however other things may acquire temporary importance—but the soul. And so will love in the Christian be like the love in that divine life out of which it springs.

IV

(*B*) LOVE AND STRENGTH

Side by side with the law of love we set the correlative law—the law of strength. It is, in one way, another aspect, or perhaps a qualification, of the law of love itself. In his relations with his fellows, the Christian man is to be no flaccid sentimentalist, no obscurer of moral distinctions for the sake of peace; nor is his love for his brethren to betray him into mere slackness, or into a constant mildness of attitude which does not change whatever the moral situation of the moment may be. In his very love he is to be strong.

Falling back upon our regulative conception, we see at once how the call to be strong issues therefrom. The Christian man is to bear himself after the dictates, and according to the impulses, of the divine life within. And in any action initiated from the indicated source or in any action adjusted by the Christian himself upon the lines which he thinks the impulses and dictates of the divine life would appoint, there could be nothing of that mere complacency to which good and evil are the same, nothing that savours of compromise with wrong, nothing of that moral feebleness which is so frequently mistaken for a grace. The divine life, transfused with love though it be, cannot look upon sin save with a frown: the Christian, did the divine life wholly make him, would therefore avoid any blinking of the dark colours of sin as he would avoid sin itself; and the Christian, seeking to govern himself (in the absence of a perfect government by the divine life) according to the idea of what the divine life would do, must be prepared to be sometimes strong as well as gracious and tender toward his fellows—knowing, indeed, that strength such as this, the strength of mood and judgment called out by the presence of wrong, is an essential part of the truest love.

Basing itself upon other considerations, starting from another point, love not seldom forgets to be strong. Indeed, any one with a taste for epigram might summarise the present mood of many people, in regard to their relationships with their fellow-men, by saying that it is a mood of no real sentiment, but of much sentimentalism. Love of a positive order, love which cares too much for those whom it embraces to be afraid of plain dealing, love which precisely in proportion to its greatness refuses to be blinded to moral character or to ignore moral distinctions—this is a thing comparatively rare. Love which has sickliness for its most prominent feature, which deprecates any raising of the voice and shuts off any expression of indignation, whatever the moral conditions may be—this love, so called, has settled itself in occupation of the minds and hearts of not a few. True sentiment towards others, which means a realisation that between our lives and those of our fellow-men a channel must be kept open for the passage of the emotion really called for by each moment as it comes, has been lost: sentimentalism towards others, which means that we must have no relation with our fellow-men save such as is implied in offering them sweets, holds the field. At all points of life the same idea emerges. There must be no reproof, else the reprover is unbrotherly. Nothing louder must be permitted than a very mild dissent from even the most obviously wrong courses. Discipline, whether in home, in school, or in prison, must have no sting. The very idea of anger or penalty is looked upon as belonging to a barbaric age. All round there is the cry for a smooth softness of bearing, for a general arrest of judgments, for a conception of mutual relationships which makes the suppression of all except compliment the supreme duty of man.

From our standpoint—and remembering what

has previously been said as to the moral quality always inherent in love of the true order—the mistake of such a spirit at once becomes clear. With a love that is reproduced from, or conformed to, the love in the divine life, mere sentimentalism has nothing to do. As a supposed revelation of love, the spirit of sentimentalism is nothing less than absurd. For love always contains within itself the hope and intention of ministering to the good of those loved—to their good, not merely in the sense of their happiness, but in the sense of their moral enrichment. Love does not leave the loved life alone simply because interference may hurt: before anything morally inferior in the loved, love will recognise it and be roused; and any love worth the name knows that the working out of its ideals will sometimes mean the infliction and the endurance of pain. There is a place for a right antagonism in a true conception of the Christian man's relations with his fellow-men. Love itself requires it. The Christian, amid all the movements of tenderness which he will ceaselessly feel, will still be strong; and his strength will issue not from an impulse contradictory of love, an impulse which divides with love the empire of his nature, but from love itself. It will be an essential part of love's very life.

If one turns to the example of Christ, love at

its highest is perceived to be strength no less than grace. He cared for peace. He came to make peace. Prince of peace—we are not wrong when we call Him by that name. But He cared only for the peace which follows upon the victory of the good; and any peace which came from a blotting out or an ignoring of moral distinctions was a false peace in His eyes. We know how He thundered out denunciations against wrong wherever He found it, how He called men hypocrites when hypocrites they were. The Christ who was Love could sometimes wield the sword. He even declared that it was not peace, but the sword, that He was commissioned to send across the earth— and rightly read and understood in its proper connections, the saying must be taken as one of the clear and commanding guide-posts to an appreciation of the ministry of Christ. He took sometimes the high tone. And in this, as in all other things, it should be enough for the disciple that he be as his Lord. It is no proof of Christian grace that all men applaud our graciousness. It may be a sign that graciousness, as men understand it, has left no room for grace. It may be a far clearer token of Christian graciousness that certain types of character hate us. As the Christ Himself was first of all king of righteousness, and *afterwards* king of peace, so with the Christian must the sequence run. Love may be the fulfilling of the law, but it is equally true that an assertion and an enforcement of law may sometimes be the best fulfilment of love. And, when this is so, the Christian, not because he ceases to be love, but because love in him claims to perform *all* its tasks, must show himself to be strong.

V

It is true that this doctrine may be perverted and abused. The spirit of strength and antagonism, which would rise up only on fit occasion if the divine life were in entire government of the Christian's ethical activities, may, inasmuch as the Christian still retains something of ethical initiative in his own grasp, show itself when it ought to sleep. Yet, if the *idea* of the divine life within, so far as the *fact* of it is not in being, be allowed to be regulative, the danger of perversion and abuse will at least be minimised, if not thrust wholly aside. The antagonism, the resentment, toward any man that moves in the life of God, could be only the jealousy of Eternal Holiness for itself and for its claims; and the antagonisms and resentments felt by the Christian man must never be of any meaner quality at their heart. Christian anger, Christian resentment, will be exercised on behalf of Goodness and of Right alone, not on behalf of self; and therein will be its distinction, and thereby will it be kept pure. From the Christianised heart, in the degree in which it is really Christianised, *personal* resentments drop away; and Christian antagonism toward offence goes out, not so much upon the person by whom the offence is wrought, as upon the evil by which the offence has been inspired, and which has for the time being taken possession of a human heart. He who, at the dictate of the true spirit, chooses the sword rather than peace, will be jealous, not for himself, but for the honour of Right in the hour when it is assailed, and will be foe, not to the transgressor, but to the spirit of evil which has made the transgressor its prey. And thus one comes upon the reconciliation, if any reconciliation be necessary, between the law of strength and the law of love. The true Christian antagonism, since it is not for himself that he who experiences it will be concerned, can love its enemies, be willing to stretch a helping hand to them when they need it, can bow down always in service while steadfastly refusing to silence its testimony or to slur over the claim of Right. The truly Christian heart, while often accepting as a sad necessity its severance from some with whom it would fain be at one, will nevertheless keep unimpaired those reserves of love which will at the first touch of opportunity throw it back into union and fellowship once more.

Treating the matter of the Christian's relations with his fellow-men as a question of spiritual biology, relating the ideal in this matter to the one supreme ideal, asking how in this matter the Christian would act if a divine life were manifesting itself through and developing itself from the ethical activities of every hour, we reach then the conviction that in the Christian man love must be married in closest union to strength, that, indeed, in the Christian love and strength are one.

VI

(C) The Christian and Judgment of Others

Out of what has been said arises the question of the Christian's judgment of others—how far it is permissible, on what lines it may run, what its limits may be. If the Christian is at any time to take up an attitude of unflinching antagonism toward his brethren or toward some quality in his brethren, something in the nature of estimate and judgment is necessarily implied. What is the order and rule which estimate and judgment are to observe?

The first and most obvious thing to be said is that, when the Christian bears himself as he would bear himself if the divine life within possessed the entire governance of his ethical activity, judgment of others will be a real estimate, not a mere process of finding fault. For it is thus, we know, that God's life in us, reproducing so far as is possible within the limitations of our nature the judging processes of God Himself, would order the matter. God takes the *whole* man into the reckoning. Judgment, with Him, is no mere searching for flaws. God really knows men. If, in the statement that God knows the thoughts and intents of the heart it be implied that He perceives all the heart's secret failings, it is implied also that He perceives all the heart's hidden good. And the Christian man has never a title to pounce upon a suddenly discovered fault or flaw in his brother, to take it as significant or representative of his brother's character, and from the single wrong conclude that he knows all there is to be known It is not thus that the divine life would act. Judgment, when the Christian exercises it, must be estimate, "appreciation" in the full meaning of the word,[1] not a mere finding of fault.

The man who claims to "know men" is in this matter very often at the opposite pole from that at which the Christian should stand. He who declares most loudly that he knows men gen-

[1] In the sense in which Mr. Walter Pater, for instance, employs the term.

erally possesses nothing more than a keen eye for the failings of his brethren, and has no adequate conception at all of the positive elements out of which a complex personality is made. He claims—perhaps with truth—that by no one would he ever be taken in: he would never mistake a bad man for a good, nor be blinded by a superficial glamour; but that is really the sum and substance of the knowledge whereof he makes so large a boast. And it is, in truth, no knowledge at all. To detect the weaknesses of any character is most assuredly not to understand it: no character is made up of one quality alone, whether that quality be bad or good; and it is at least possible, when the evil has been discovered, that a further investigation might show it to be of much less importance, in proportion to other things, than it seems to be when taken alone. To know a man is to weigh each element in him, not separately, but relatively to all the rest—to recognise where the morally emphatic place of his nature is when all the facts have been allowed for—to see how many votes in the government of his life every different quality in him possesses. He who, with one rapid glance, singles out the worst element in another, and then passes on, can make no claim to know his fellow-men. He has caught one splash of colour on the picture, and has decided that it offends his eye; but he knows nothing of the grouping and proportion and scheme of the whole. He may be quite correct in his estimate so far as it goes; and yet the fact that it does not go far enough may vitiate it through and through. To know the worst about a man is not to know the man himself. And to the Christian man, striving to find the line on which his judgment of his fellows would be driven if it issued out of an entire surrender to the divine life—to him all these considerations, obvious as they are even on the ground of common sense, will appeal with tenfold power. For the divine life would judge, not a part of the man, but the whole.

If, indeed, we apply to this matter the *complete* formula under which our thought is working, it will become still more evident how utterly the spirit of mere fault-finding fails to carry it out— or rather, how that spirit makes it impossible to carry it out at all. The divine life within is to manifest itself in, dictate to, and *feed itself upon* all the ethical activities of the Christian's days —the ethical activities involved in the Christian's relations with his fellow-men, and in his judgment of his fellow-men, among the rest. And the Christian, in so far as he adjusts his ethical activities for himself, is to adjust them as though this process were being carried on. But it is impossible for the divine life to *feed itself upon,* to *develop itself through* the Christian's relations with his fellows if, in his judgments of them, he has an eye only for their moral rents and scars. For it is implied in this attitude that he is always on his guard, never receptive, never susceptible to impression, never open to any ministry which might come upon him from his brethren. The interaction between life and life is non-existent for the man who is ever on the watch for fault. There dwells in him none of that generous willingness to receive which, no less than a generous willingness to bestow, is one of the marks of a Christian soul; and, inasmuch as he is looking for nothing else than evil to come from those he meets, he has no use for any gift of grace they may have to offer. He cannot be himself the better for his contacts with his fellow-men. As a matter of fact, experience and observation supply evidence enough that the "man who knows men," or thinks he does, who lives without any real mutual relations between himself and the rest of the human family, becomes morally smaller as time goes on. He is almost always, from the standpoint of character, shrivelled and gaunt: of real moral greatness he has none, irreproachable as his record may be in respect of actual wrong-doing; and one knows that beneath the shell of this moral crustacean no sort of evolution into a higher grade of life is going on.

And the same principle holds good when it is a question of the distinctively Christian life, not the ordinary moral life alone, feeding itself upon and developing itself from the Christian's relations with his brethren. Only through a judgment which seeks to see the whole, can any reaction of good be obtained from the character that is judged. If this is to be done the Christian must make his judgment of his fellows a real *estimate,* so far as it is possible, not a mere finding of faults. It is thus that the divine life within him would judge; and it is thus that the divine life within him would establish and strengthen itself through its contacts with men. It is by a real "appreciation" of his fellow-men that the Christian makes them minister to the good of his own inner life. The Christian, therefore, working by the regulative idea of the divine life within, treating the question of judgment as a question of spiritual biology, will, for the sake of his own spiritual profiting, as well as for other reasons, reckon up men's *positive* qualities, or will endeavour so to do, and will be exercised to discern in others, not alone the evil, but the good as well. For it will be his business really to *know* men—and only in this wise can men be known.

VII

On the wider question whether the Christian is to be at liberty to exercise any judgment of his fellow-men at all, there is one decisive thing to be said. If his relations with his brethren are ordered in part by the dominance of the divine life in him, and if, for the rest, he seeks to order them as though that dominance were complete, he will undoubtedly be moved at times to frame some verdict upon what others do. In so far as the very life of God occupies the field within him, it will be in itself a test of whatever approaches, and will be consciously realised as such. But, at the same time, the Christian, however complete may be his surrender to a life-power higher than himself, is not delivered from the limitations of knowledge whereby man is necessarily beset; and from this fact follows the qualification that, while he may judge what his brethren do, a judgment of what they *are* he is never at liberty to make. Even a perfect dominance of his own personality by the Personality of God would not bestow upon him the final and infallible knowledge which belongs to God alone. And to pronounce a verdict as to what his brethren, in the inner make of them, really are, is therefore wholly beyond his possibility and outside his sphere.

The distinction between judgment of what our

fellow-men do and what they are is a distinction easily appreciated and, for that matter, easily kept in mind even amid the multifarious contacts with our brethren into which we find ourselves compelled to enter. Certainly it is a distinction which the man who strives for a really Christianised ethical ordering of his life will write clearly upon his heart. It is quite impossible for any man immersed in the common activities of common life not to have an opinion concerning the worthiness or unworthiness of some particular concrete action which another man close at his side suddenly puts forth into the world to which they both belong. Human lives being so closely bound together, and what is done by one acting so powerfully upon other lives than that of the doer himself, no one can help framing some deliberate estimate of his neighbour's doings as they emerge into the light. And, in so far as the divine life makes the Christian, or so far as he calls in the idea of an indwelling divine life to be regulative of his spirit and his mood, the Christian's estimate will be legitimate and at any rate approximately true. This judgment—followed, if circumstances require, by an expression of it—is certainly a permissible thing. It will issue naturally out of the constitutive elements of the Christian's nature. But he who passes from a judgment of what his brother *does* to a judgment of what his brother *is*—who presumes to make, on the evidence which this or that action supplies, a final decision as to his brother's moral condition or status, and determines in his thought the precise place in the moral ranks his brother is fitted to occupy—takes upon himself a function he has no qualification to discharge. However far the making of the Christian by the divine life, or the regulative influence of its idea over him, might be carried, the faculty for such judgment as this would not be conferred: indeed, just in proportion to the extent of the divine life's sway within him or over him would the Christian sheer off from any attempt at a final reckoning up of his fellows, since he would have a true consciousness of his limitations as well as of his power. This arrest and limiting of judgment would issue naturally, as the previously mentioned positive judgment would issue naturally, out of the constitutive elements of the Christian's life. To estimate how good a man is *in himself*—to assert that because he does this or leaves that undone he must be just this particular distance from the Kingdom of Heaven—to settle his position in regard to the eternal standards of character— shows the arrogant, censorious spirit of judgment to which the Christian man has no right to yield room. In this sense, he must not judge, lest he himself be judged. The Christian man will remember that he knows but a few of the facts which go to make up his brother's moral life. There are a thousand points he knows nothing about, on which he would need to be enlightened before he could have any just opinion concerning his brother's moral health. He will take into account the fact that a man who commits a wrong may be *essentially* better than the man who avoids it. He will admit his own ignorance as to the wrestles the erring one may have gone through, as to the temptations he may have endured, as to the initial inherent weaknesses of disposition which may have handicapped him in the moral race. And, remembering all these things, he will, while ready to declare, when the declaration is required, that this or that action is right or wrong, avoid passing anything like a final sentence upon any transgressor or fixing his precise place in the moral scale. Ordering himself according to the conception of a divine life manifesting itself in all the activities involved in his relations with his fellow-men, the Christian will be frank upon what his brother *does,* reticent or silent upon what his brother *is.* For it is thus that the divine life, working within and through a human mind and heart, would have the lines of estimate and judgment fixed.

VIII

(D) THE CHRISTIAN AND INFLUENCE

An integral part of the question of the Christian's relations with his fellow-men is the matter of his influence upon their moral life, of the degree in which he is responsible for the exercise of such influence, of the method in which it should be put forth. Important as the matter is, however, it may be said that from our present standpoint it settles itself; and to see that it does so settle itself is the best result we can reach through whatever study of it we may make. Treating it as a question of spiritual biology, thinking of the Christian as one in whom a divine life is manifesting and developing itself, one sees that out of the Christian an influence and a spiritual ministry naturally issue—not so much because he seeks to make them issue as because he cannot help it. And the point for the Christian is not the elementary one, "How far am I committed to an active ministry of moral and spiritual benefiting towards my fellow-men?" but the deeper one, "Is there going out from me the active ministry of moral and spiritual benefiting which, if I am a Christian indeed, will be an automatically-wrought consequence of the life within?" On the point of influence, in fact, the Christian has not to bring what goes forth from him up to the measure of what, when judged by the measure of what is within him, he thinks it ought to be. He has rather to take the measure of what goes forth from him as the test and measure of what is within.

The true Christian experience necessarily passes beyond the limits of him who possesses it, and makes an appeal to other lives. And it does this, as previously said, simply in virtue of what it is, and because the thing cannot be helped. The presence of a divine life in any man means that something distinctive begins to pervade the whole nature, something which, simply because it is there, speaks and appeals, something which becomes so much a part of the man's personality that, wherever the personality is recognised at all, *it* is recognised also. Since personality, character, is the one thing we are always impressing upon those we meet, the divinely-transfused and divinely-transformed personality and character must do a changed work and act in altered ways upon all around. Just in proportion as the Christian ideal approaches fulfilment *within* us will it suggest itself in everything that passes *from* us; and as it is impossible for the sun, charged with light, to come within range of human vision without making men conscious of its shining, so is it in the very nature of things impossible for a nature charged with the divine life (even though in imperfect measure) to come within reach of human hearts without making them conscious that it is there. It is character, the whole moral constitution of us, that is ceaselessly stretching forth its many hands to touch and shape our fellow-men. We may know things, and may not open our lips to tell them: we may own things, and keep them back from others' eyes with a miser's care; but character is the one thing we cannot choose but show to others, and the one thing which others cannot choose but see and feel. It is admitted by all that atmosphere—the strange, subtle influence which comes out of the depths of character, which never says anything and never does anything, but which is the essential revelation of personality—is a thing far more important and far more powerful, too, than definite words uttered and concrete actions done. Whoso is made by the divine life will carry always with him, diffuse ceaselessly around him, an atmosphere which must be felt. Even with other things it is so. Your man of refined and lofty pursuits and interests—your cultured man—bears with him his atmosphere. He is not always talking learnedly, or actually unloading his own intellectual goods in order to bestow them upon less favoured minds; but the culture which makes him shows itself in almost his lightest word—a thing not to be defined, but clear enough all the same. The suggestion of culture leaps from him, let the immediate matter be what it may. How much more must it be so with those who are in true submission to the life of God. The divine life possessing a man must make all life a suggestion of divineness; and the divine atmosphere—if it be in the house of character at all—must fill even the commonest room. Like that subtle chemistry the ancient sages sought for, which, had it been found, would have transmuted all common metal into gold, so the divine life within a man must make life's commonest contents shine before the eyes of men with something of a golden heavenly glow.

Certainly in the earthly life of Christ Himself (and, as was said, we find Him in a very intimate way to be our example throughout the whole of this realm) things were so. Just because He was what He was, He pressed ceaselessly upon men the appeal of another life and another world. It was not that Christ had something special within Him which He revealed now and again and then hid away once more: He had been so sent by the Father that out of the very make of His being the missionary appeal and the ministering testimony came forth. When He spoke, and not less when He was silent— when He laid men under the spell of astonishment by some marvellous work, and not less when He permitted His power to lie in rest—always and unintermittently He was, simply by the life in Him which could not be hid, suggesting, persuading, warning, presenting life's finer ideals, and wooing men thereto. His very silences must have been eloquent: His very presence, though it did nothing but pass by swiftly and quietly and go as a breath is gone, must have been so spiritually fragrant that none could choose but heed. And as the Father sent Him, so would He send His own. He, bringing into us the life of God which dwelt in Him—He, making us one with Himself as He Himself was one with God—would have us to be so re-made through that union that there shall be a positive and unmistakable suggestion of higher life emanating from us, be our outward attitude and occupation for the moment what they may; and He would have His disciples be surrounded always by a spiritual halo which shall speak to men about, and appeal to men on behalf of, heaven and goodness and God.

It is from this point, and along this line, that the Christian should approach the question of his influence upon his fellow-men. It is not so much that he has to make or create an influence by some effort of his own. The point is rather that by the influence he is actually exerting *without* any effort of his own he may test his own measure of divine life. It is not putting the matter strongly enough to say that he who is truly a Christian will be moved to go forth and touch the world with what influence he can. It is not the consequence of being a Christian, but actually a part of it, to diffuse what is received over those who have it not. The Christian needs first of all to approach the matter of influence in indirect fashion—to remind himself that it is in the automatic influence of character that he ought, in the nature of the case, to be most rich. He has to remember that just as the lamp becomes incandescent when the electric current passes through, so, without effort, must character become spiritually incandescent when the divine life passes along all its fibres. And, for the rest—when he remembers that only in limited degree does the divine life possess him and make its appeal through him—he will at least endeavour to appeal to his brethren by an ever-quickened longing for a deeper experience (since this, like the deeper experience itself, cannot be hid, and is one of the most penetrating spiritual ministries in all the world), and, if he cannot speak to men through the beauty of holiness, will speak to them through the beauty of a desire after holiness which is at least in process of being fulfilled.

IX

The correlative suggestion, along this line of thought, is a suggestion as to the effect which the Christian may expect his influence to have upon those who come beneath its sway. His influence, as we have seen, is primarily the influence of character, of life; and it is upon character and life that character and life will do their work. That is, the Christian is not necessarily to influence other people in the direction of ordering the external activities of their lives for them, but in the direction of suggesting a spirit which will enable them to order their own. The Christian, treating the question of his influence upon others as a question of spiritual biology, must be content to forego the pleasure (as human nature holds it) of bringing other lives into an outward conformity with the pattern of his, and be satisfied with bringing near to other lives a spirit and a life which, when his brethren receive it, must be left to work itself out in them as it will.

It is probably a native instinct with the majority of men to want to give actual detailed advice or instruction to other people, and to reckon the amount of influence they are exerting by the degree in which they can succeed in bringing other minds to accept their doctrines, or in getting other courses of action discarded in favour of their own. Yet to lay too much stress on the measure in which these results are attained is to confuse a spirit with the effects worked out by the spirit; and it is surely a far greater and nobler thing to call a right spirit—the spirit of love for the divine life and of consecration to the divine life—to call that into being within another nature, even though that spirit should choose for the manifesting of itself ways that are not ours, than to obtain a mere mechanical conformity of another's action and opinion with our own. The influence of character upon character is one of the greatest things this world contains: the quickening of a right spirit in another man is a better thing than the mere instructing him as to what, in this emergency or in that, he is to do; and this is the task which is committed to the Christian's charge. It is thus that the Christian's commission must be read. He has, with the character in him transformed, with the atmosphere that makes him re-created out of holier elements—he has so to reveal the transformed character that those whose character is yet untransformed may realise the miserable sordidness of theirs, so to diffuse the re-created atmosphere of personality that others shall feel how much is lacking to the sweetness of theirs. Not to make others do as he does, but to make them see something in the life out of which his doing springs—that is the

Christian's line. Not to influence others in the sense of causing them to take his external activities for a model to be reproduced point by point, but to influence others in the sense of convincing them that the inward sources whence the activities come are purer than any they possess—that is the Christian's line. And let it be added that in this view the hope of influencing others becomes possible for all. We cannot always advise others, or instruct others, so complex and various are the circumstances into which any one may find himself thrown, and so little may we be able to grasp the conditions among which our brother has to thread his way; but the suggestion of a right spirit can always go forth from us to struggling spirits near by. In this way, the smallest life, the life which in one sense knows the least, may give impulse to the life that is greatest and the life that knows the most.

One sums up the matter by saying that the influence of the divine life, acting through the Christian man, is simply in the direction of suggesting the necessity for an in-dwelling of the divine to the Christian's fellow-men. So does the ideal of the Christian's ministry shape itself—and brief as the expression of it is, no nobler ideal could be. For as we remember that He who said, "I am the light of the world," said also to His disciples, "Ye are the light of the world," and as we ask ourselves how this thing can be—that we should be what the Master was—we see that it can be only in this way. But in this way it can be. By our suggestion of the divine life as the supremely necessary thing, we begin the shining into other lives of that Light which has shone into our own, content, thereafter—if we be disciples indeed—to let other lives be kindled, not at the light in us, but at the Light whence our own is derived. It is by caring before all things that his influence shall be an influence of character upon character that the Christian does what he can to bring human lives into contact with and submission to the life divine.

VIII

THE CHRISTIAN AND DISCIPLINE

UPON our present line of thought, the question of the Christian's relation to the sorrow and pain of life—to the whole sum of experiences which goes under the name of life's discipline—becomes a part of the ethical scheme. The Christian's concern is no longer about compensation for, but about obligation in, the seemingly sadder elements of his lot. It is not from the ethical standpoint that this topic is usually approached; and yet it is inevitable that it should be so approached, if the regulative principle by which we are working be applied all round the circle of life. There is to be, in the Christian man, a divine life manifesting itself in, dictating to, and developing itself from, all his relations with the world and with the life coming to him through those relations: he is at least to adjust himself as though this were being done; and this programme is not fulfilled for him unless, while he passes along life's darker valleys and rougher roads, he bears himself as one who not only endures, but conquers, as one who not only comes

THE CHRISTIAN AND DISCIPLINE

out unscathed, but as one who is in truth the greater and the better for the journeying that was superficially so hard. Clearly, it is on the fact that the divine life is to *develop itself from* the Christian's connection with all that befalls, that the emphasis must in this connection be laid; for the only action the Christian can take in regard to the heavier experiences of life is to secure whatever *reaction* of good they are able to afford. And, when he asks himself what his attitude is to be amid these things, the Christian must therefore put the inquiry as one that bears, not so much upon a comforting for which he hopes, as upon a duty which he has to discharge. It is, in fact, as we shall presently have occasion to repeat, because Christian men and women so often approach the matter from the idea of consolation for trouble rather than from that of duty in trouble, that consolation itself fails to arrive. Applying our regulative formula, we see at once that the question of the Christian's attitude toward sorrow and pain belongs to the range of questions embraced in the Christian ethical scheme. And it is no superfluous thing to recover into the ethical atmosphere and to the ethical plane an aspect of the Christian life that is treated too often from lower points of view.

How, then, from this standpoint, is the Christian to bear himself when life's clouds gather and upon life's ways the going is rough?

I

He must, for the first and primary thing, recognise the *positiveness* of all the experiences of his days. He must hold that every experience, whatever its outward aspect may be, is not something lying outside the directly elevating ministries of life, only brought within them, if at all, by a sort of corrective exercise of God's power, but is in itself the direct offer of a gift. For this, surely, is how the divine life, dwelling within man and ordering all man's attitudes and moods, would view the diversified stretches of experience: it would look on all things as welcome, as positive in their actual offers and in their possible effects; and it would be, not defensive, but aggressive and eager, in regard to all. And to this method, consequently, must the Christian conform.

Commonly, we fail to attain to the height of such a spirit as this. We tend to assume that only one part of life arrives straight from God, and with God's direct commission to bless: the other part, although it may, by some sudden exercise of God's almighty power, be prevented from hurting us, really comes with an originally hostile possibility and intent: what is obviously pleasant and enriching we recognise as such, and

THE CHRISTIAN AND DISCIPLINE

say "This is God's gift"; but the rest—the experiences which visit us without a smile upon their faces and wearing perhaps a look of mystery which we cannot penetrate—the rest, however God may subsequently turn its harmful power aside, is not primarily a minister of grace. A portion of our living of direct sacred origin, and a portion of an origin that is not sacred— so our fancy shapes it; and if only that which is not of immediate heavenly birth can be prevented from poisoning us with its baneful influences, there is no more for which we can hope. Our faith—what there is of it—gets on the defensive so quickly, when there arrives some experience which does not seem at once to fling forth its benediction into our grasp; and, while we willingly *receive* one section of life, our prayer is to be *saved from* the other. The divine *positiveness* of life we do not always apprehend.

The true Christian attitude is a much more strenuous and a much larger thing. That no element of life needs to be a wasted thing for him, barren of any inspiring suggestion or unable to enrich—still more, that no element of life can be in reality opposed to him, an enemy from whom he runs away to hide in coward fear or whom he entreats the power of Heaven to smite down before too much harm be done—that expectancy will find an answer in every single thing which befalls—that all the hands with which experience touches him are hands stretched out, not to take away, but to give—these are the certainties which should be ceaselessly ringing, like peals of joyous music, in the Christian's ears. Never is it to be his request that this or that should pass him by, lest the burden of it prove greater than he can bear: rather is he to embrace and welcome and snatch at every new offer that experience makes, strange and mysterious though it be, sure that it contains within it some golden treasure it must yield up. And not that he may be able to *endure* life's darker visitations without repining—not so should he shape, not to that should he limit, his prayer. But that he may grow the richer through them all, since that is not too great a miracle—that is to be his hope and aim. Not content is he to be with the merely *negative* good of not being the worse for aught he goes through, but resolved upon the *positive* good of being better made, better built up, better endowed, by it all. And his faith is to possess sufficient quality and sufficient heat and sufficient glow and spring to assure him of this—that all life can be made to respond to his positive expectation with positive gifts.

That is the Christian attitude. And it is an attitude, be it remembered, which as a matter of *duty* the Christian is called upon to take up, since

THE CHRISTIAN AND DISCIPLINE

the regulative idea for him is that the divine life is to manifest itself in and to *develop itself through* his connection with all that befalls.

II

Emphasis must be laid, however, upon the fact that it is good of the spiritual order—an actual development of the life within—that the Christian is to look for as the result of his severer experiences; and he is not rightly adjusted to these experiences until it is on gain of this kind that he is bent. The divine life is to develop *itself* from all the passing incidents of the Christian's experience—that is, the Christian is to be better, rather than happier (except, of course, in so far as to be better always means to be happier in the long run) for all he goes through. And this brings us again to the point previously made—that the inquiry as to a right attitude in trial must be taken as bearing, not so much upon a comforting for which the Christian hopes, as upon a duty which the Christian has to discharge. And it is through our forgetfulness of this that even the comforting for which we look frequently fails to come.

The classic passage in the New Testament brings out clearly the fact that it is for a spiritual profiting out of trouble that the Christian is to be chiefly concerned. " We know that to them that love God all things work together for good," the Apostle Paul declares in tones of ringing triumph;[1] and the many who quote the words so insistently should at least be sure that they quote them in the sense in which they were first employed. Out of the significance suggested by the word " good " the moral and spiritual element must on no account be dropped, if the phrases of victory are to be used as Paul used them—for, indeed, the moral and spiritual element is the chiefest thing of all. It is not primarily good in the sense of happiness, but good in the sense of the morally and spiritually good, that all things are to work. The apostle is really stating in other language that the divine life in the Christian man is to develop itself from all the Christian man goes through, is, in brief, stating our regulative principle in this particular one of its applications. If one needs evidence that this interpretation is the interpretation consonant with the apostle's intention, one can find it, first, in the particular Greek word employed; and next, in the fact that Paul immediately passes on to supply a clear indication of his meaning by speaking about being " conformed to the image of the Son."

We get at the precise meaning of Paul's utterance, consequently, if we render it " to them that love God all things work together for *goodness.*"

[1] Romans viii. 28.

There is, or ought to be, for the Christian man, a spiritual education in all and a spiritual profiting to be obtained from all; and the purpose which life through all its range can be made to serve by those that have the true spirit in them is the purpose of enlarging their hearts' endowment of all that is worthy and noble and true. And it is for *this* gain out of seeming loss that the Christian man should ceaselessly look.

The Christian attitude toward sorrow, pain, disappointment, loss, and all the other constituents of "discipline," is not truly taken until this is realised. The true Christian attitude is certainly not taken when Christian men and women look for some magic to be worked in life for them whereby all these darker experiences will be made *in themselves* different things for them from what they are for other people. Even the Christian mind so often translates "good," in the classic passage referred to, as if it meant "pleasantness" rather than "worth." All things are to make for our good—that is, we are going to find, now or later, something pleasant come out of them for us, spite of the unpleasantness which at the immediate moment they bring. They really make for our good—that is, the Christian man ought not to feel hurt when these things strike him; and if he could only rise to his privileges, he would find their severity to be only a phantom of his imagination. He does not, of course, formulate in set words any such ideas; but in his heart he carries a vague notion that the Christian disciple ought to find no meaning in the words sorrow and disappointment and bereavement and pain: somehow, through God's manipulation of them for him, their essential character should be transformed. And, as was said, it is precisely because the wrong expectation is entertained that expectation goes unfulfilled. The Christian man finds that grief approaches with as swift a step as ever, that sorrow spares not a single stroke, that the shadow cast by death's wing is still as wide and deep.

He cannot take in his hand anything that has resulted from all he has gone through, and say "*This* is the promised good." He has mis-read the requirements of the position—mis-read the promise of it too; and hence his disappointment comes. He had no title to anticipate that when his trial was over he would be able to reckon things out and find that there was a larger balance of pleasantness than there was before the trial began. All this is far from the attitude prescribed by the idea that a divine life is to manifest itself in and *develop itself through* the Christian's contact with the harder elements of his lot. It is to good in the sense of spiritual enrichment, of character-growth, of soul-sweetening and of greatening and purifying of the heart—it is to that the conception points. And it is to this gain, and this gain alone, or at any rate this gain primarily—leaving gain of all other kind to come, if it come at all, incidentally and by the way— that the Christian who rightly adjusts his mood and attitude among the heavier passages of life will direct his expectant gaze. Living by the one regulative idea, he will pass through all fair fields of joy if there his path shall lead him, and through dreary wastes of sorrow if that be the appointed lot, and through the very valley of the shadow of death at last, as one resolved that through it all the heart shall be made truer and character shall grow. And this is the attitude, let it be said once more, which as a matter of *duty* the Christian is called upon to take up, since the regulative idea for him is that the divine life is to manifest itself in and to *develop itself through* his connection with all that befalls.

III

But it may be asked whether it is really possible for the Christian man to preserve, amid the darker experiences of his days, such an attitude that these experiences shall be compelled to minister to his spiritual good. Of course the divine life within him, did it possess all its power, would secure the desired end; but, in so far as the thing is a matter of self-adjustment, so far as the Christian still has to order his ethical activities for himself, how is he to become the spiritual master of his lot?

The answer can be given, in connection with this particular department of the Christian ethical order, as it was given to similar questions in other departments before. In the Christian man, the wish to set himself as God's life within would set him if it had all its will, has a dynamic force that makes for its own fulfilment; and he who desires to be morally and spiritually the better for the discipline he goes through cannot fail to find his desire crowned. And, indeed, in this particular instance it is easy to see that it must be so. To say that he who wants to grow through experience is sure to do so, is but to enunciate in other terms the constant law that all life tends to feed and to confirm whatever is the ruling element in a man's character, the law which is always being proved in a thousand instances before every observant eye. The effect which the experiences of life produce in us depends upon that in us with which they come in contact: there is not a single joy and not a single sorrow which affects two people in precisely the same way: the nature in them takes up the experience as it comes, is worked upon by the experience and itself works upon the experience, and strengthens itself in whatever its dominant quality may have been by the experience as it passes by. The predominantly mean and ignoble man will rise for a moment to sun-lit heights of joy, and the joy will only minister to his meanness: or he will be clasped for a moment in the arms of sorrow, and the sorrow will but fling him out of its embrace presently meaner and more ignoble still. The predominantly great-souled man will climb to those same summits of joy and submit himself to the clasp of that same sorrow, and will come down from the mount of delight and emerge from the embrace of grief with a yet more fulfilled greatness in him, with the moral quality of his being strengthened and confirmed. And in the classic Pauline passage just now referred to, the apostle is really basing himself upon this unalterable law. "We know that to them that love God all things work together for good." It is not simply a categorical statement which Paul had himself accepted, and which he desired his readers to accept, in a spirit of unquestioning faith. It is the summing up of an argument which Paul has at the moment no time to draw out in its fulness. The reasoning behind the assertion—the reasoning implied, though not expressed—is that love or desire is a power which forces all life and experience into the service of its own ideals, and that love, directed upon God, must, therefore, force all life and experience into the service of goodness. Which is but another method of saying that all experience feeds and strengthens the moral quality and desire which has been uppermost within. All things work together for meanness to him who loves what is mean. All things work together for greatness to him who loves what is great. The Christian, as he seeks to adjust himself in the true attitude amid the disciplinary trials of his life, and wonders how he may make sure of not missing the discipline, may rest in hope upon the law. His desire for it tends unfailingly to fulfil itself. The love of good is the love of God—and to them that love God and good all things work together for good. They meet the sorrow which would narrow and belittle another, and, because care for nobleness is supreme in them, the sorrow works out in nobleness. They are touched, as others are, by the finger of pain, and, though to them pain is pain still, the soul takes no hurt thereby, but, because care for all great qualities is supreme in it, grows the greater for the very pain. He who keeps the love of good alive in all its strength—who keeps the heart aspiring toward good with all its power —who keeps the passion for good palpitating through every fibre of his moral being—will find that to his predominant love of good all life, whether for the moment it wear its robes of gladness or its sombre garb of grief, whether it come with gifts in its hand or with a sword to destroy what he has held most dear, will answer with the longed-for good. In this, as in all else —and in this realm perhaps more obviously than in many others—the wish to set ourselves as the divine life within would set us if it had all its will, has a dynamic force that makes for its own fulfilment. And in that unalterable law the Christian of true and earnest purpose may rest.

IV

In one way, this particular application of the Christian ethical method enables the Christian to test himself, his own spirit, his own depth of Christian temper and mood. The degree in which the thought of a spiritual profiting through trial appeals to us may be taken as a test of what we are. The Christian man may well ask himself whether he cares enough about being made good to be satisfied with the assurance that to that end all things are tending if he will have it so. Or does he want to fall back upon the meaner "good," and have God weigh out to him enough of pleasantness to make up for what he goes through? He may be sure, of course—even as the apostle, austerely bent upon spiritual ideals as he was, would have avowed himself sure—that at the long last there would be pleasures for evermore at God's right hand, that in heaven the perfect gladness on whose face he never looks for more than a moment here will lift up the light of its countenance upon him ceaselessly, that there his buried delights will rise from their graves and come to meet him in all the glory of resurrection, that there his heart, which has hoped only to find hope's blossom wither in the east winds and which has aspired only to droop wearily, will be satisfied, that there all the discords change to sweetest music, that there his dear dead ones will be folded once more in his arms. But he must know, also, that all this is, in its fulness at any rate, only for those who care for the higher "good" most and first. Is he content that it should be so? Or does he want to bargain that for every treasure taken from him he shall be paid back in similar kind? By the answer his heart gives, he may test his spiritual quality and his Christian rank.

At any rate, it is to this distinctively ethical view of life's experience, and of their true attitude beneath it, that Christian men and women need to come back. They must rise beyond those exercises of faith which simply declare that trial is God's will, that for all the hardship of life they will be amply repaid in the end, that things are better than they seem. They must set themselves to making life's harder elements a discipline indeed—a positive ministry of positive good. They must recover into the ethical atmosphere and to the ethical plane this department of the Christian life which has too often been treated from a lower point of view. And it is as a matter of absolute *duty,* let it be repeated, that this is to be done; for the regulative idea for the Christian man is that the divine life within him is to manifest itself in and to *develop itself from* all that befalls.

IX

SUMMARY—THE INCLUSIVE RULE

IT is not necessary to pursue the application of the general ethical method of Christianity into other departments of Christian practice. What has been said as to the Christian's relations with the world, the Christian's relations with his fellow-men, and the Christian's bearing under the discipline of life, will serve as sufficient illustration, and will enable the reader to see how in other spheres the same principles may be worked out. As in the spheres dealt with, so in all the rest, there is to be the governing fact—or, in so far as that fails, the governing idea—of a divine life manifesting itself in, dictating to, and developing itself from, the ethical situation in all circumstances that may arise. We pass at the close to see if there be for the Christian man any inclusive rule in which all that has hitherto been said may be gathered up.

I

Before doing this, however, it will be as well to recapitulate briefly the attained results of our thought. And it is thus the summary will run.

The ultimate ethical ideal, according to Christianity, is not that a man should know how to bear himself in any crisis of experience, and should act out his knowledge, but that he should bear himself rightly without thinking about it—almost as if he could not help it: in the final condition to which the Christian scheme looks forward, the moralist is lost in the saint. The distinctly religious programme of Christianity, both in what it prescribes as the sum total of man's spiritual adjustment, and in the subordinate and temporary programme which it imposes in the absence of the perfect thing, keeps this ultimate ethical ideal in view; and in so far as man pursues the religious programme, he pursues ethical perfection too. Even in its lower and intermediate stages, the Christian programme views the inner religious life and the outer practical life as in closest relationship, and presents man as being ceaselessly engaged in a spiritual development that is going on within—a spiritual development that must have ethical consequences—and as reaching forth to life's ethical problems only out of that development, in such fashion as that development prescribes. The relation which is absolute unity at the highest stage of Christian experience is at least to be maintained as action and reaction while the lower stages are passed through. As a matter of fact, however, the Christian is compelled to attack many ethical problems as it were *in themselves*—not primarily in their relation to his inner spiritual life, and out of his consciousness of his inner spiritual life, but rather as separate objects in the field of experience; and hence he needs some further guide. The daily programme for him, therefore, as the practical problems come knocking at his door, is this. He must, at each emerging crisis, realise himself afresh on the side of *being*, call on the divine life within him, in its actuality and in its potentiality, to become regnant over the position, so that it shall be, not he, but God present in him through Christ, that deals with the question and decides the way. And by this is not meant simply an effort of imagination: what is meant is rather an actual movement of the Christian's own life and of the Christ-life within him, a movement that swings each to its proper place, bringing the Christ-activity, in place of the Christian's self-activity, to the directive post which it ought always to have, but from which the too assertive self-hood of the Christian man frequently keeps it away. So far as possible, it is the actual divine life within the Christian that is to direct and rule; and the Christian must, at the coming of every practical question, so re-adjust himself spiritually that this may be. The function of conscience in the Christian man is to proclaim whether or no this has in any particular instance been done. Yet, when it is done, surrender to the divine life is still incomplete: the fact of the divine life is not entirely regnant as it ought to be; and something of initiative yet remains in the Christian's hands. For the right guidance and ordering of this, he is to call upon the *idea* of the divine life within, and is in all things to control his ways as he believes the divine life within would control them if it had all its power—his reckoning out of his conclusions being at least in measure guarded from error, inasmuch as the divine life does truly make and constitute him in part. He has but to make an extension for himself in thought of a line which experience has already begun to draw. He is to treat every practical problem as a problem of spiritual biology. So is the relation between the inner life and the outer still maintained. So does the Christian, in even the smallest concerns of life, relate the ideals to the ideal. That, dealing with practical questions thus, he may sometimes come to conclusions similar to those reached by other ethical methods, we have seen. But for him the whole thing will be rationalised: the precepts by which he lives will stand upon a different and a definite basis, will be no longer arbitrary or disjointed, but will be realised as organically bound up with the spiritual processes which constitute the Christian's true life, and will in consequence be more binding and more energising by far. And, to what was previously said about the action of conscience in deciding whether, in every practical crisis, the Christian has, so far as he could, substituted the decisions and activity of the divine life within him for the decisions and activity of the self in him, it may now be added that conscience supplements this ministry by declaring whether, in the absence of the perfect regulation by the *fact* of the divine life, the *idea* has been duly called upon to rule. Once again, the formula may be set down. The Christian man has to remember that, according to the proper ordering of things, the divine life is to manifest itself in, dictate to, and feed itself upon, the ethical activities of every hour; and in his own ordering of things, so far as any remains to him, he must act as if this, and this alone, were being done.

II

But if it be said that all this seems to make the Christian ordering of life too complicated a thing, and that on this method Christian ethics becomes too stringent a task, what answer can be given? If some simpler statement of the Christian ethical programme be demanded, can one be found? One might say, of course, that the suggested programme is after all not so complicated as it

SUMMARY—THE INCLUSIVE RULE

appears, and that the processes of ethical adjustment here prescribed are, like a good many other processes of the moral and spiritual life, accomplished as it were in one flashing movement of heart and mind, although many slow movements of speech be needed to set them out. But, in point of fact, a simpler statement of the Christian ethical method is at hand, though only now, at the end of our previous thinking, could it be properly made or understood—a statement in which all other things are embraced, a statement which may be taken as the inclusive rule for the Christian's conduct amid the practical concerns of life.

At each emergence of crisis, the Christian must call up the living presence of the living Christ, and submit himself to its spell. So the inclusive statement will run. It may be objected that this is merely one of the commonplace phrases of a fervent and unthinking evangelicalism, and scarcely gives out the ring of a serious treatment of the important theme at present in hand. One of the phrases of a fervent evangelicalism it may be; but it is certainly none the worse, no less appropriate and suggestive, for that; and it is certainly the phrase which precisely describes the one necessary thing. And, at the point we have reached, though perhaps only at that point, it can be adopted with discernment of its significance, and without risk of the misunderstanding, or the inadequate understanding, of it into which a fervent evangelicalism sometimes falls.

It is true that something like "realising the presence of the living Christ," "entering into communion with Christ," "going out to Christ in submission and faith," is often advocated as the solution of the Christian's ethical perplexities by many who give no rational account of the way in which ethical assistance is supposed to be derived from the process, and who indeed almost resent the suggestion that any rational account of it can be given. And the process itself is often conceived as if it were merely an emotional recognition of the fact that Christ is near—a mysterious ethical dynamic following, in some thaumaturgical fashion, upon the emotion's birth. By this emotional recognition the Christian conscience is supposed to be quickened, the good more clearly discerned, the impulse toward it made to beat with redoubled speed and power; and in proportion as the Christian works himself into warmth of feeling before the present Christ, finds himself up-lifted into something like rapturous delight, ethical possibilities are enlarged. But the *rationale* of the supposed ethical enlargement is too seldom apprehended, however earnestly the need of realising the presence of the liv-

SUMMARY—THE INCLUSIVE RULE 243

ing Christ be pressed; and perhaps it is not unjust to say that, in many presentations of the matter, the radical flaw lies in attaching more importance to what goes out to the Christ from the Christian than upon what comes down upon the Christian from the Christ. "The apprehension of the living Christ" is the phrase; but the accent falls upon *apprehension* rather than upon *Christ*. And the apprehension is taken almost as a piece of magic whereby the Christian is enabled to overcome ethical difficulties which were too much for him before.

At the point to which our thought has led us, we can employ the phrase just given as embodying the inclusive ethical rule, with an adequate apprehension of its meaning, and with an adequate apprehension of its reasonableness besides. The Christian, at each emergence of crisis, is to call up the living presence of the living Christ, and to submit himself to its spell. What is meant is that, whenever problems of practice press, the Christian is to realise the living Christ, the Christ in whom the actual dynamic of the divine life always dwells as close at hand, and is to let the dynamic issuing from that Christ take grip upon him afresh. It is not a matter of thinking about Christ as He was till the historic Christ seems to project a vision of Himself upon the canvas of the present moment and to stretch a hand down across the years. It is not a matter of working up warmth of heart and mind and soul before a sort of vividly-imagined Christ, till the vividly-imagined Christ reacts with beneficial inspirations upon the heart and mind and soul which have imagined Him. It is not a matter of realising Christ *as if He were here*. It is a matter of knowing that just as I *am* here, so He *is* here, with life in Himself and with the creative power toward me implied in that word—and a matter of permitting His creative personality to enfold my own. The Christian, at his hours of ethical stress, is to realise the living presence of the living Christ.

And the reasonableness of this as a method of mastering the ethical crises of life is easily seen. It is strictly in line with all that has been said before. What the Christian has to do, we have seen, when the problems of conduct present themselves, is to set himself in such an inward attitude that the divine life within him may win increase of power and may take governance of the situation with which the Christian himself knows not how to deal. But it is through the Christ— through the dynamic of the living Christ—that the divine life will win that increase of power, just as it was through the dynamic of the living Christ that the divine life in the Christian first began; and to say that the Christian is to set

SUMMARY—THE INCLUSIVE RULE

himself in such an inward attitude as shall secure for the divine life within him increase of power is but to say in other words that he needs to subject himself anew to the magnetism and mastery of the living Christ. The Christian surmounts his practical problems, therefore, by calling up the living presence of the living Christ, and submitting himself to its spell. It is no piece of emotionalism that is thus advocated: it is no thaumaturgical device that is thus relied upon: it is actually the scientific method—one need not fear to put it so—of grappling with the ethical difficulties of life, this method that is here set down. Or if we pass to the further point of the programme previously drawn up—that the Christian, in so far as the *fact* of the divine life fails to be completely regulative of his ethical activities, is to summon the *idea* of it as a supplementary regulative power—we can similarly declare that by calling up the living presence of the living Christ and submitting himself to its spell, the Christian carries the programme through. The Christian's own thinking about the true course—his own effort to ascertain what line of action the divine life within him would impose if it had all its power—becomes reliable and safe, at any rate far more reliable and safe, becomes indeed more largely possible in many cases where it was almost impossible before (since in some instances of moral crisis the very greatness of the crisis seems to paralyse the necessary thought) if the Christian sets his mind under the direct dominance of the mind of Christ. He may not be able to make the entire surrender of personality to the living Christ which, by substituting the very life of Christ for his own, would cause the divine life to govern the situation with unfettered power; but if he realise the living Christ as actually there, such measure of thought as he is still compelled to take, such degree of moral self-adjustment as he is still, in the absence of a perfect surrender, compelled to perform, will win something of success and worth from the influences radiating out of the Christly presence. When, therefore, we say that the Christian, in so far as the ethical ordering of his life remains in his own hands, is to govern it under the regulative idea of the divine life within, we do but say in other words that he is to govern it under the sway and spell of the mind of Christ. The *mind* of the Christian may be in great part submitted to the *mind* of Christ, even when it would be too much to say that the *life* of the Christian, as a whole, is Christ's and not his own. The Christian surmounts his ethical problems, therefore, by calling up the living presence of the living Christ and submitting himself to its spell. Again, it is no magical pass across the ethical difficulties of life

SUMMARY—THE INCLUSIVE RULE

that is so suggested, but a strictly reasonable method of dealing with them all. For all other rules this one all-inclusive rule can be substituted. In it all the rest are wrapped. And the Christian who has taken hold upon what has been written through earlier chapters may now say (since he will now understand what lies behind and what is implied in the saying) that the whole ethical programme is summed up in flinging himself into Christ, heart into heart, mind into mind, soul into soul, *life into life*. It need not be denied that they who employ the phrases concerning the "living Christ" in the method not unfairly to be described as the method of magical incantation, who think of the proper attitude towards the living Christ as one of heightened emotion and sublimated ecstasy—who, in brief, lay more stress upon what goes out upon Christ from them than upon what comes down to them from Christ—it need not be denied that they obtain for the ethical governance of their experience something of the help for which they hope. For, after all, the living Christ *is* there; and the life-influences starting out from Him come even upon human natures not properly prepared or set, and do something of their helpful work. But the Christian who, in his reliance upon the "living Christ," knows the ground of his reliance, knows what he expects, knows how the descending life-influence is to do its work and why it is this life-influence that above all he needs—he will obtain far more from the living Christ than the surrender of mere emotionalism can ever win. And so we repeat that, while all that has gone before stands sure, the Christian who has properly apprehended the method of his ethical safeguarding may now substitute this one rule for all the rest, and may determine to master all his practical problems by calling up the living presence of the living Christ and submitting himself to its spell.

III

There remains little more to be said. But let it be noticed that in this way, and in this way alone, is Christ brought into touch (as ah! so many Christian men and women are ceaselessly longing, and vainly longing, to bring Him into touch) with all the practical problems of our day. It makes a veritable heart-ache, sometimes, for earnest and devout ones to realise that the swift movement of the world in which they live, the kaleidoscopic changes among the conditions of their own individual experience, are carrying everything further and further away from the world and the experience to which Christ appears to belong, and that from His world and experience to their own lines of connection are becoming ever more and more difficult to draw. The problems of life increase in complexity, and He said so little that touches them. Nine-tenths of our horizon does not seem to have been within His view. There is no word for this, for that, for the other situation that baffles us. And yet we cannot go through all these things without carrying in our hands some talisman which is His gift, which will open for us all the doors. If we once confessed that we had to do so, it would be a confession that our Christ had failed, that He is not the Christ for the present day. Even while mourning that Christ, as He was, seems somehow out of relation with the practical problems of life, men and women refuse (with an intense passion which shows that they hold themselves, not Christ, to be wrong) to believe that He is really so. And, pathetically, they strive to bring Christ into relation with the conditions of the newer time. They talk of imitating His example, only to find that in many ranges of life no example was given: they endeavour to discover in His utterances general principles which will cover the special matter perplexing them, only to find that the method satisfies neither them nor any others involved in the case. In a hundred ways they seek to make the desired contact between Christ and the modern time. What if Christ be making it Himself, or ready to make it?

What if He said so little, because He intended to *be* always what He was then—the Source of a life under whose tides of power all practical problems would be directly overcome? At any rate, under the view we have been taking—the view which finds in the realisation of the living presence of the living Christ, and in submission to its spell, the entire ethical programme for man, whether as individual or as member of a social organism—under this view Christ becomes the direct arbiter of the modern world, and will retain His place as such through all that may happen in the process of the suns. So much, at any rate, is gained.

And this, too, is a helpful word. If this ethical method be accepted, then the ultimate ideal (the combined religious and ethical ideal) is forwarded for the Christian man by his grappling with each practical problem as it comes. As he faces each problem, he seeks so to fling himself into the grip of the Christ-life, coming down upon him out of the living Christ Himself, that the divine life within him shall decide his course. And in so far as this is only incompletely done, he seeks at any rate to be so united with the living Christ that such adjustment as he has to make shall, through the dominance of his mind by the mind of Christ, be taken nearer to truth and worth. But this closer union with, or this

SUMMARY—THE INCLUSIVE RULE

closer approach to, the divine life in Christ must necessarily mark a *permanent* gain—not, perhaps, that the high tide of fellowship with the divine life which was reached at the moment of crisis will be maintained, but that the tide will not sink quite to its former low level again. It is in the nature of things that the *special* effort at surrender which, under the stress of the crisis, the Christian has been driven to make, should cause the *normal* measure of his surrender to be enlarged.

So, by every practical crisis, rightly confronted, is the Christian carried nearer to the ultimate goal—the goal of having no life save that of God through Christ within him, all practical crises being consequently done with and passed by. So is there an inter-relation between all the affairs of life—the smallest question of conduct, once met and conquered, contributing something to the Christian's equipment for hours of larger import and keener stress, and all together, through the successive alternations of life-power gained and used and increased through the using, making for that final issue of things wherein all the ethical ideals shall be automatically realised in the realisation of the one great spiritual ideal. On this view it is upward and onward always, and through the smallest movement of experience no less surely than through the greatest—the Christian mounting ever on stepping-stones of his past self to higher things.

IV

The reproach of mysticism may perhaps be raised once more against this ethical method at the end. Well, what needed to be said as to the precise relation between mysticism and practical affairs was said on an earlier page. But for the rest, let it be admitted that mysticism of a sort all this undoubtedly is. And it is mysticism unashamed. In the last resort, all that has been written depends upon the real livingness of Christ to-day—upon His continued possession of creative power. It depends, therefore, upon such mysticism as this may imply. If Christ be only a memory—only a historical Figure that passed once, grand in moral stature and sublime in moral example, across the world's stage—then it would be useless to speak of calling up the living presence of the living Christ; and, with the going of that, all else in these pages would be gone. But if Christ be really, not in any metaphorical or poetical sense, but in all literalness, present still among men, not as the great dead of the human race are present, but in far more intimate ways—if it be true that it has been given Him through all the ages to have life in Himself—if He can unite Himself with men, heart with heart,

SUMMARY—THE INCLUSIVE RULE

thought with thought, will with will, soul with soul, *life with life,* till His personality folds itself close round theirs, substitutes itself for theirs—then all that has been written may stand. It is mysticism, perhaps. But it is a mysticism which is, as some of us would hold, vital both to the Christian religion and to any sound Christian ethical scheme. It is a mysticism which is the most practical thing in all the world. And it is between faith in a Christ who *was* and faith in a Christ who *is* that those who call themselves Christians are being more and more insistently called upon to choose.

In the interest of a sound ethical ordering of life, no less than in the interest of a rich religious experience (for indeed the two are, as repeatedly emphasised, really one), it will need to be the Christ who *is* that the Christian retains for his worship and his trust. So is it, in the last resort, the divine life, in its fact or in its idea—ever less and less in its *idea* and ever more and more in its *fact*—that orders the ways of the Christian man. So is it possible for him to see to it that a divine life within him shall progressively manifest itself in, dictate to, and feed itself upon, all the ethical activities of his days. So does he relate the ideals to the ideal. So does the man of deepest spirituality become the man of swiftest and truest aptitude for a correct dealing with practical affairs. And so does the mystic, the saint, wrapped in Christ-ward adoration, absorbed in Christ-ward communion (so that it be a communion wherein the *whole* man moves out to the *whole* Christ, and the *whole* Christ comes back upon the *whole* man) find himself, through the energising power of that life-sacrament whereof he ceaselessly partakes, thoroughly furnished unto every good work.

THE END